WE THE VILLAGE

T0151891

WE
THE VILLAGE

ACHIEVING OUR COLLECTIVE GREATNESS NOW
THROUGH STUDY GROUP VISIONING PROCESSES
LEADING TO ACTION

Ramona Hoage Edelin

THIRD WORLD PRESS

Progressive Publishing Since 1967

Chicago

Third World Press
Publishers since 1967
Chicago

© 2014 Ramona Hoage Edelin

All rights reserved. No part of the material protected by this copyright notice may be reproduced, stored in a retrieval system, or transmitted in any form by any means, electronic mechanical, photocopying, recording or otherwise without prior written permission, except in the case of brief quotations embodied in critical articles and reviews. Queries should be addressed to Third World Press, P.O. Box 19730, Chicago, IL 60619.

First Edition
Printed in the United States of America

Library of Congress Control Number: 2014946737

ISBN 13: 978-0-88378-329-0

18 17 16 15 14   6 5 4 3 2 1

Cover Art by Reginald Harmon
Cover design and interior layout by Relana Johnson

To my Ancestors
who found the light in abject, man-made, darkness
and used it to illuminate our path
to righteousness and uplift

To the young adults
who so fervently want to see the light
and implore us to share its brilliance with them

To Alma Mater,
Fisk University,
where I again received the light from the Ancestors
and learned to direct its powerful bright beam
onto new paths
and hold it steady

CONTENTS

ACKNOWLEDGMENTS

The contents of this volume have been subjects of my scholarship, teaching, mentoring, policy development, leadership, and the establishment of the cultural foundation of my home and child-rearing practices for more than forty years. At many points over the years, loved ones have asked me to produce a book for them. I am so grateful to those who encouraged, prodded, and, in one or two cases, even threatened me, to get it done. I hope it is "right on time" —even though it is quite late by some accounts.

My deep gratitude to Bernard C. Watson, Abena Joan Brown, Aileen Hernandez, and the late M. Carl Holman, cannot be overstated. Their support of my intellectual development and leadership, their unwavering admonitions that I must write this book, and their willingness to share their great wisdom and truly vast experiences with me undergird my belief and clarity immeasurably.

My students and the young adults who have participated in the leadership development programs I have created, inspire me continually. Special thanks to Tony Menelik VanDerMeer, Cheryl Wright Grills, Ron Lester, Brian Johnson, Meta Williams, Maurice Carney, Kelly Owens, Trabian Shorters, and Esther Benjamin, for their particular interest in probing group-conscious cultural leadership with me. For my friends the late Ronald Walters, Adjoa Aiyetoro, Rico Speight, Ethel Mitchell, Juliette Bethea, and Louise Olivi, whose encouragement has been steadfast through the years, I have deep gratitude.

The technical support I received for this volume from Michelle Bragg, Rhett Lewis, Nancy Freeman, Charlotte Reid, and Marlene Johnson and the cover art by Reginald Harmon was indispensable and is very much appreciated.

Before all, my family is my rock. Without the timeless foundation of the love, choices, sacrifices, tutelage, nurture, correction, protection, discipline, networks, lessons in self-sufficiency, faith, and confidence of my grandparents, William Charles II and Alethia Lightner Lewis, and my mother, Annette Lewis Hoage Phinazee, I would not know in the deepest sense that I do, what Village even means. My late uncle and his family, and our entire extended family, continue to help me preserve and sustain the values of the Ancestors for and with my children and grandchildren. It is my children and their families — Kenny II, Kimberley, Ramad, Charlisa, Kendall, Clyde IV, Kenny III, Caleb, Kimi, Kayla, Christian and Cheyenne, whom I love so profoundly, for whom I live and learn.

INTRODUCTION

Taking a step back. The 2008 political season presented the United States with an opportunity to look without turning a w a y immediately, and to hear without tuning out instantly, at race and ethnicity. T h e n United States Senator Barack Obama's success as an African American in winning the presidential nomination of the Democratic Party, and in being the first (acknowledged) African-descended person to win the United States Presidency, overcoming the assaults, slings and arrows of a long, bruising campaign and the centuries-old legacy of race stigma, is historic in the most profound sense.

President Obama's great accomplishment led some commentators and leaders to question whether the U.S. has arrived at the point of being "post racial," meaning race is no longer an issue for the nation; and whether the time of African Americans making what could be considered reasonable political demands based upon race has passed. Despite the brutal and in many instances obviously racist opposition the incumbent faced in the 2012 election, this question somehow persists. "There's no point in dealing with the whole race thing anymore."

On the contrary: this is the best time for us to complete the work of finally eradicating the caste stigma of race and color—which are still very much alive and are felt each day in the lives of the overwhelming majority of our people! No political figure—even the President of the United States—can solve all problems of race alone. President Obama will need us to do the great work of racial and cultural uplift that *we* need to do, so he can make the greatest advances that can be made from high office. Only the enormous power of our collective will to advance our race can facilitate what we need to do in our own homes, schools, faith centers, organizations and communities. Only the enormous power of our collective will to advance our race can give the Leader the outside propulsion he will need in order to prevail on the inside. A critical mass of change agents is needed right now!

We need to step up our game in the same way that Barack Obama stepped up his game! If each and every one of us, with all our many and varied gifts, talents, and specialties, would step up like Barack has stepped up, our race would be in a very different condition! What is our agenda? Who has to do what, in order to make it happen? What can and should we be doing to improve the quality of life for African-descended people in the United States? What are the policy implications of our goals and objectives that a political leader could promote? It's time to break it down and tighten it up!

"Perfect and unlimited equality" is what Dr. W.E.B. Du Bois envisioned for us. Can we begin to envision it for ourselves? What would be different in our own minds if we believed this? Can we act like we already have it? Can we construct our agenda and conduct our collective affairs as though we are, indeed, the perfect and unlimited equals of any group on earth? Can we get unstuck from our entrenched negative preoccupation with racism, oppression, economic exploitation and caste inferiority—even while they still exist in the nation and the world; even as we plan together to end them? Can we give our attention to group uplift, rather than to anger and a total focus on how wrong and unfair our treatment has been? Can we overcome the searing, debilitating pain? Can we be positive and affirmative about the advancement of our group, at this historic time? Yes, we can!

When this author proposed a Cultural Offensive beginning with consistently referring to ourselves as African American in December of 1988, it was for the purpose of flipping the script.[i] Rather than dragging along behind on the defensive, we would surge forward on the offensive. Rather than referring to ourselves as a color, we would identify ourselves correctly in a geopolitical context and name the land of our origin. Any African-descended person living in the U.S. was welcome to share this identity. Group consciousness begins with identity. Group consciousness was and is needed in order for us to use our culture as the vehicle for the advancement of our group.

An African proverb has captured the imagination of this nation and has traveled to other parts of the planet. "It takes a whole village to raise a child" made its way into political discourse at a time when certain populations of young people were in peril and few real solutions were being advanced. Among African Americans, in the 1980s, one of every two children under six years of age was officially born into poverty. Hunger and homelessness, crime and substance abuse, disease and ill health, and appalling low academic achievement were out of control. **Our children asked the most difficult questions that can be asked of a group:** *"What difference does it make whether I live or die?"*

No unified response was forthcoming from leaders and other adults, and these young people started to look only to one another for answers. Hip Hop culture, at first a strong, progressive demand for relief from police oppression and economic devastation, quickly grew deep roots and branched out into other expressions. When it finally became undeniable that the whole village was needed to fulfill its duty, the stunning romantic impact of the Ancestors' proverb was irresistible.

Yet, we must admit, we have permitted the proverb to become merely a metaphor, just as we have permitted the conditions under which our children live to become intolerable. We did articulate and mount an African American cultural offensive in the 1990s. Together with the economic gains of the Clinton/Gore administration, conditions did improve in that climate. However, conditions have reversed again; and it is clear that a sustained program of development and uplift is needed from a defined village with an effective cultural blueprint.

This group must control its destiny no matter who sits in the White House or in the seats of leadership in the Congress, State Houses, and municipal government. The question now is: what will we do to become that village? How will we arrive at a coherent, lasting intellectual infrastructure out of which practical and moral group decisions and action will ensue? How will we BE that village, now?

*****

What are the biggest problems we need to solve? Why are our economic realities so grim, all over the world? Some point to **education,** because without a world-class education neither we, nor our young people, can compete in the twenty-first century as thought leaders or in the global labor market. Others focus on **health,** because without good health learning, earning and personal productivity are diminished. Others make **politics** their priority, because public policy frames and determines so many resource options in society.

These factors are obviously vitally important, but this author maintains that any African-descended person who is not actively engaged in group-conscious efforts to change our condition has a conscious or unconscious death wish. No one wants to live a life of degradation, inferiority, with no way out. The death wish can be seen in depression, rage, risky health and safety behaviors, anti intellectualism, antisocial lifestyles leading to incarceration, violent patterns of domestic interaction, homicide and suicide. **Therefore, I contend that the biggest problem we need to solve is that of getting connected to and resurrecting our cultural offensive—our Movement.** When we share a great vision of the uplift of our race and work toward achieving it together, we experience an empowering sense of purpose. This was certainly true of our Movement in the 1940s, 50s and 60s—in fact, it has been true going all the way back to our enslaved Ancestors. It must be true again! With a high purpose, no problem is too large; without purpose, any problem is too large.

How do we resurrect our cultural offensive, our Movement? This study will not answer these vitally important questions—no one person can or should presume to establish a group agenda unilaterally—but it will raise them, and give them historical and cultural referents, with the hope that we, as a group, will begin to think about them, deliberate, make decisions and plans in keeping with our decisions, and move toward becoming the village we so desperately want to be, and many know we must become. Consider it a guided "visioning process"[ii] through which we forge the thought leadership of a critical mass of African-descended people to bear on achieving our collective greatness now.

The setting is a Study Group of young adults who see themselves as emerging leaders. In Study Groups, facts and ideas are taken from history, current events, and personal experiences, to contribute to the rich and deep understanding of what is being studied. In this case, the need for African American Cultural Renewal leading to the construction of twenty-first century environments that do for the race what the ancient Village did, is the subject of study. Guidance will come from the dialogue and also from extensive footnotes and references to other documents and materials that the Reader may choose to explore. Study Groups study! They can also move from study to the application of what they learn and come to understand, to well-informed, collective action.

This volume is compiled and written for, and dedicated to, the young adult leaders and young adults with whom I have worked over the last forty years, and this cohort globally, who want so much to know what the Movement was and is, and what their roles in its advancement can be. It seeks to fill some voids, answer some questions, and ask some. It is meant to help build the foundation you need in order to lead the Twenty-first century movement.

It is a story about a study group that came to think of itself as the Mission Inevitable team, and how, in seeking to answer the desperately important Question of one twelve-year-old boy, it envisioned and built a cultural Village.

Our Ancestors organized themselves, focused their concerns into explicit agendas, spoke truth to power, and demanded authentic change and improvement for our group time and time again after we reached these shores. They envisioned a future based upon what they did want, rather than what they did not want. Their excellence and sacrifice have prepared the way for us. We must not falter and we will not fail!

WE
THE VILLAGE

One
BUDDY

"What difference does it make whether I live or die?!"

Buddy's rage and despair engulfed the small kitchen and silenced his family's voices, minds and hearts. The twelve year old youngest son was in trouble at school, at home, and perhaps soon with the law. His eyes, once bright, were now cold and dark; his mind, once sharp and astonishing, was now fixed in a negative downward spiral; his spirit, once aglow with promise and confidence, was now mean and foreboding. He was angry and abusive. He could not make sense out of anything. He was afraid. The Question he shouted through burning tears and a convulsing stomach demanded an immediate and coherent answer: *"What difference does it make whether I live or die??!"* At that moment, his devastated family did not have the answer.

***

That was eight years ago. Beginning that day, his older brother Sol insisted that Buddy join him in a study group that was working on a project bigger than anything the community had taken on before. He was not the only junior partner in the effort—several of the planners had also decided to include their younger siblings and extended family members, boys and girls, who were demanding answers to the most important Question that can be asked of a culture; who were exhibiting signs not only of self-hatred, but of a death wish.

The study group gave itself the name Mission Inevitable (MI) when it decided to undertake the project. The MI team believed the answer to the Question, and to the destructive world view and belief system the young ones were experiencing, was systematic cultural renewal and actually building the community that would embody and sustain it. Buddy met Sol's closest partners that first night, and they let him know very directly that answering his Question was the most important thing in the world to them.

The MI Team

Ra was the leader; you could feel his power and presence in a room even when you were not looking at him.

Herma had all the news and analysis of current events; she tied everything to decisions political leaders would make or should make.

Tom had doubts about everything everyone else said; but he would think fast about what it would cost and how to get it done once he was convinced.

Marguerite. Buddy had never met anyone as passionate about justice and fair play as Marguerite—and she talked about spiritual powers that were different from what he heard in church.

Buddy sat next to Sol and Ra; and Buddy could hear them going over certain points just between the two of them. Sol was around twenty-two years old and Ra was a bit older. Ra talked about who we are and why it is important for us to think and act as a group. Buddy paid close attention to Ra because Sol seemed to look up to him, and because what he said was strong.

The MI team always met at a lady's house, and she always offered them something to eat and drink. Her home was full of art and books and it made Buddy feel more at peace. Her name was Aida and Sol said the whole idea of the study group was her program for them when they were younger. He said she had vision, and she cared about young people more than most other adults who could have been helping us. She was always there, but she almost never said anything unless a MI team member asked her something. When she talked, Buddy felt like he was in the presence of wisdom. And he knew she really liked him, just by the way she looked at him.

Aida was a daughter of the civil rights movement who spent her formative years living on the Historically Black College campuses where her grandfather and her mother worked. She thought she would always be a teacher and she became a third generation college professor; but later in life she focused more on policy and politics because she wanted to sustain change as well as help to create it. But she always kept younger emerging leaders nearby, through her leadership development programs, through mentoring, and now by way of her study group. Back in her day, children and young adults were active players in the Movement that changed the world; and she had been among the student leaders. Her love and respect for young people were deep and manifestly obvious. With all her education and experience, she always said she learned more from her students than they did from her. She could see more than we thought we were showing, and hear more than we thought we said—because she cared so much for us

When Buddy and Sol got back home late that night, Buddy realized the pendulum of his emotions had swung from extreme pain to extreme contentment in one day. There was an answer to his Question; and his big brother and the MI team were helping him to understand it!

The Mission Inevitable (MI) Village

Today, the MI Village is nearly complete. It's like a campus. Housing for children in foster care and their caregivers is completely renovated or newly built as green, smart buildings complete with Internet connectivity. Each house accommodates eight children and four adults. There is affordable housing for staff, teachers, community police officers and other caregivers. All government services can be accessed in the Services Center, and there are people who help families figure out what they need. Lots of businesses and service providers have chosen the campus as one of their locations. The main house, MI Central, has a dining room and restaurant, library and computer lab, game room, meeting rooms, the Boardroom, and an auditorium. The library and computer lab are open twenty-four hours a day, and people from the community are always in there studying, taking online courses and tests, and getting a GED (general education degree). Community groups use the meeting rooms all the time; and there are rehearsals, performances and plays in the auditorium almost every night. The school and athletic fields also get lots of community use. MI Village has a residential center for young mothers and their babies, from birth to three years old; a school for preschoolers through sixth grade; a middle school for sixth through eighth grade; and a high school. The allpurpose athletic field is home field for baseball, football, soccer, and lacrosse teams; the indoor and outdoor basketball courts are all in use all the time; there are four outdoor tennis courts; a swimming pool, and a great golf course. The MI Village invites the community and lots of important people out to the Games and performances; and the restaurant is the favorite gathering place for everyone who is part of this movement for cultural renewal. The gardens, and the agriculture and aqua-culture sites and renewable energy centers now being planned, are the talk of the town.

The network of caregivers, educators, lawyers, social workers and service providers, artists and activists of MI Village provide alternatives to incarceration for first-time non-violent offenders within the village; parenting help; elder care; and training in community organizing. Everyone in MI Village can answer the Question. Buddy is now one of the assistant coaches for the athletic program, and he manages the afternoon study groups for high school students.

Two

DEFINING AND ESTABLISHING THE CULTURAL CONTEXT

Behind, beneath and before human thought and action in any current generation lies a great body of group experiences, choices, adaptations, knowledge and inspired wisdom from the Ancestors in preceding generations, centuries and millennia, whose force and power is too little understood. This incomparable tool for human development and group advancement has been studied by anthropologists, sociologists, philosophers, theologians, psychologists and sometimes by political scientists, but rarely as it obtains, or could obtain, to current conditions and affairs in Western societies. It has been given different names over time and space, but, for the purposes of these studies, WE THE VILLAGE, we will call it culture, define it, and establish the context for its use.

Study Session One

Ra has focused intently on cultural renewal because he is convinced it is the key to personal mastery and group consciousness. At MI study group meetings, culture is all he talks about. He is soft-spoken and thoughtful; and he has an advanced degree that credentials him to teach at the university and write reports and essays. He is not what anyone would consider handsome, exactly, but there is something very compelling about him. He has what Sol calls charisma. Ra opened with this statement:

"Culture is the total way of life of a people"

Culture is the total way of life of a people: the values, the rituals and spiritual demonstrations, the patterns of thinking and deciding, the commerce and enterprise, the proclivities and choices as expressed in music, folklore, literature and art, the habits and tendencies as recorded in group history, the institutions, socialization processes, systems of rewards and punishment, the identity of a group, as compared and contrasted to others.[1] While we are today not particularly conscious of the cultural dimensions of our lives, these dimensions are present and await our group-conscious use of their enormous potential for good.

Tom said he is not particularly conscious of it—he just wants to get paid, and he wants to stop seeing so many poor people in our group. What does culture have to do with that? Tom is a budding entrepreneur. He wants to beat the system and make it work for him; and he is sometimes embarrassed by the poor and the excuses they give for their condition. Sol asked Tom to hold on—all will be revealed to him if he will just hear Ra out—even though he has heard it before, let Ra present it another way. Marguerite agreed, and pressed her view that culture has a spiritual dimension that is necessary for development, including economic development. Herma said she needs a research-based solution in order to get the politicians to relate to the MI team's approach.

Setting a Foundation
Ra continued: Dr. William Edward Burghardt Du Bois (1868-1963) is revered as the creator of the Black Intelligentsia[2] largely through his strategic and purposeful use of the communications organ of the National Association for the Advancement of Colored People, *The Crisis* magazine, which he founded in 1910 and edited until 1934. His purpose was to explain and illuminate group identity, group consciousness, and group empowerment. We look to his *Conservation of Races* for a riveting declaration: "the history of the world is the history not of individuals but of groups, not of nations, but of races, and he who ignores or seeks to override the race idea in human history ignores and overrides the central thought of all history." What, then, is a race?

> It is a vast family of human beings, generally of common blood and language, always of common history, traditions and impulses, who are both voluntarily and involuntarily striving together for the accomplishment of certain more or

less vividly conceived ideals of life. Turning to real history, there can be no doubt, first, as to the widespread, nay universal, relevance of the race idea, the race spirit, the race ideal, and as to its efficiency as the fastest and most ingenious invention for human progress.[3]

Ra paused, to let these powerful thoughts sink in. Then he continued: There is a myth, a bona fide Big Lie, in Western societies, and particularly in the United States, called "rugged individualism." It would have us believe that each of us is autonomous, making our way in the world by our own deeds and powers without any help from systems or groups, and that we "get what we deserve" in that solitary struggle. This can be a seductive, ego-stimulating concept. Most among the white majority who benefit from this view of the world keep silent even when they know better, because of the privilege that derives from it. Many among the historic numerical minority of peoples of color in the U.S. somehow believe this delusion also. Those who live unexamined lives, who have not looked behind, beneath and before surface appearances, may believe this myth, this Big Lie.

Just below the surface, however, lies a centuries-old and ever-renewing cultural corpus defined by white supremacy and privilege, by economic exploitation and political hegemony. Its systems of social, legal and economic organization, its acculturation processes, its police and military enforcement codes and practices may seem to be "just the way things are"; but they have been designed to keep one group in power, with privilege and impunity, at the expense of other groups and regardless of the price to them.

I maintain that the African American group will never take its place at the table of cultures as equal to the other great races, unless and until it regains its group identity, renews its group culture, and recommits to ensuring group progress by all culturally appropriate means.[4]

Aida got up and moved toward the kitchen as everyone soaked up Ra's passion and thought about what he said. Buddy caught it as she quickly looked at him and smiled. Tom was pensive. Herma was taking notes as quickly as she could. Marguerite had a smile that made her look like she knew a secret she had not shared with us. Sol had started to speak as Aida returned with a platter of fruit, cheese and crackers. "No matter what the obstacles—real or perceived—we have to prevail," Sol said. "We are here in America—the United States, rather—what should we be thinking about as a numerical minority of the population, Aida?" he asked.

Question: what does it mean to be a "minority group"?
Aida responded by asking another question: what does it mean to be a "minority group"? Pausing for a moment of reflection she then answered, "John U. Ogbu gives a thoughtful set of definitions in his *Minority Education and Caste* as follows"

> Autonomous minorities tend to be numerically smaller than—but not totally subordinated economically or politically to—the dominant group. They often possess a distinct racial and ethnic, religious, linguistic, or cultural identity, which may be guaranteed by the national constitution or by tradition. Sometimes autonomous minorities occupy distinct geographical domains, over which they exercise political control while participating in supralocal politics. They may be subject to some prejudice and discrimination, but their relationship with the dominant group is not characterized by rigid stratification. The ideology of innate inferiority may be completely absent in the majority-minority relationship.

> Members of autonomous minorities do not necessarily regard the majority group as their reference group, nor do they necessarily want to be assimilated. The existence of autonomous minorities as separate groups is not based on any specialized economic, ritual, or political role they may fulfill; in fact, they are usually free to pursue most social and economic activities for which their training and abilities prepare them. Autonomous minorities are found in most developing nations of Africa and Asia; in the United States, the Jews and Mormons probably best represent this type of minority group at the present.

> Caste minorities are the polar opposite. The dominant group usually regards them as inherently inferior in all respects.

Some caste minorities are more or less pariah groups. According to Berreman (1967a: 293), pariahs are low-class groups who are regarded as "intrinsically polluted and are stigmatized and excluded." Their economic, ritual, and political roles are often sharply defined. The kinds of work they do are usually "the necessary but dirty, demeaning, and unpleasant jobs for their superiors" [Berreman 1967a: 292]. In general, caste minorities are not allowed to compete for the most desirable roles on the basis of their individual training and abilities. The least desirable roles they are forced to play are generally used to demonstrate that they are naturally suited for their low position in society. Thus their political subordination is reinforced by economic subordination. Blacks in the United States, the scheduled classes in India, and the Barakumin of Japan are examples of caste minorities. Immigrant minorities fall between autonomous and caste minorities. These are people who have moved into a host society more or less voluntarily." (Mabogunje 1972; Shibutani and Kwan 1965). As strangers, immigrant minorities can, if they live in groups, operate effectively outside the established definitions of social relations. They also tend to have instrumental attitudes toward their host society and its institutions. Such attitudes enable them to accept and even anticipate prejudice and discrimination as the price of achieving their ultimate objectives.

In general, the goal of immigrant minorities is not necessarily to seek equality with the dominant group but to improve their economic condition relative to the condition of people in their homeland. The Chinese and Japanese in the United States are examples of immigrant minorities.[5]

"That's it!" shouted Herma. "As long as African Americans confine their thinking and limit their geopolitical reality to the United States, we should at the very least set our mind to achieving autonomous minority status, throwing off the shackles of caste stigma and improving the economic and political condition of the millions who are today still systematically shut out of the nation's prosperity and democratic ideals."

Marguerite asked, "Is this what Barack Obama has done? Has he been able to conceive of himself as a member of an autonomous minority? Is it because he is not the descendent of enslaved African people? Is this what is at the root of the difference in achievement between African-descended immigrants and the descendants of slaves? This is amazing!"

Tom was quick to point out that many African-descended immigrants had forbearers who were enslaved—particularly West Indians. The triangular trade included them. Yet, they see themselves differently and often do not associate themselves with the struggles of African Americans.

Sol made the observation that perhaps the key to this is in Ogbu's statement of the goal of immigrant minorities: they are not totally obsessed with achieving equality with Whites here in the States—they want to improve their economic situation as compared to what it was back at home. "We are totally focused on achieving equality, on righting a crime against humanity, on not being considered inferior and not being victims of discrimination and exploitation," he said. Buddy was thinking of some of the African and West Indian kids at school; and what they were saying was making some sense for him. They did not seem to jump on every remark, or to hear what he heard from some of the teachers that was so disrespectful. Buddy saw and heard disrespect everywhere. It made him so angry he didn't want to even go to school.

Marguerite was thinking about something that seemed to trouble her. Slowly, she wondered aloud, "Is the experience of the enslavement of our Ancestors embedded in our genetic memory, as some say? Have the persecution, the pain, and the ill-treatment become part of our DNA? It may be possible. And, if so, we need to draw upon our enormous spiritual resources to change that memory that is now a part of our genetic makeup. We won't succeed in our cultural renaissance if we can't use all the positive and constructive lessons, but get rid of all that negativity, despair, and defeat."

Ra asked Marguerite to bring information about genetic memory and the spiritual resources to the next meeting. Buddy had never heard of any of this; but he wanted to come to the next meeting so he could find out what Marguerite was talking about.

Ra continued the lesson. "When we look and see more globally, we will know the Pan African reality is not a minority position at all, particularly when we find common cause and act in solidarity with other oppressed peoples around the world. The knowledge and understanding of some of our own group's immigrant minorities will be particularly helpful in broadening our vision and sense of possibility."

A good note to end on, everyone agreed.

Three

THAT WAS THEN, THIS IS NOW

The Mission Inevitable team had an ongoing topic for study: How do we transform our group? How do we plan our group life together; devise means for using our collective resources—intellectual, spiritual, moral, technical and financial—for the good of the whole; forge strategy to undo the structural and mental barriers[1] that have prevented our advancement as a race?

Study Session Two

Ra started the deliberations with the statement, "We must begin at the beginning, with a clear understanding of identity; and then build a cultural construct that will help us uplift and advance.[2] "Who are we? Above all, it is necessary to establish the fact that our history does not begin with slavery. We are an ancient people, the first of the human species to emerge on this planet and therefore the parents of everyone on Earth. Our group sojourn has taken us from prehistory to the twenty-first century and will take us infinitely beyond this period."[3]

A prehistory Lesson

Tom had been assigned the summary of the period of study. He told the group our first Golden Age, which spanned the period of The Nubian Dynasty of circa 3400 B.C.E. through the Ptolemaic Dynasty of 323-30 B.C.E. gave us and the world the great spiritual, civic, medical and scientific mysteries of Kemetan, or Egyptian, culture.[4]

****

Another Golden Age in Ancient Sudan, Western Africa, was produced by the empires of Ghana, Mali and Songhay. Ghana dominated for almost three centuries, flourishing in the ninth and tenth centuries and reaching its peak in the eleventh century; Mali rose in the thirteenth century; and Songhay was the seat of power in the fifteenth and sixteenth centuries.[5] African people organized and governed prosperous and peaceful nations for thousands of years before the enslavement of our Ancestors.

****

Eminent historian John Hope Franklin teaches us, in *From Slavery to Freedom*[6] "When, in 1517, Bishop Las Casas advocated the encouragement of immigration to the New World by permitting Spaniards to import twelve Negroes each, the slave trade to the New World was formally opened." (p. 49) England and the United States outlawed the slave trade in 1808, but the law went unenforced in the US. (p.154) "With the official closing of the African trade in 1808 the domestic trade became more profitable; and by 1815, about the time of the great movement of the population into the cotton kingdom, it had become a major economic activity in the country. Rapidly the machinery for handling the traffic developed, and before the very eyes of Americans there emerged an institution which served as a substitute, or a supplement, for the African trade and which was only slightly less obnoxious in its effects upon the social order." (p.175). "At the last census enumeration before the Civil War, the Negro slave population had grown to 3,953,760." (p. 186). President Lincoln signed the Emancipation Proclamation in 1863. Congress passed the Thirteenth Amendment to the Constitution, abolishing slavery in The United States upon ratification, and established the Freedman's Bureau, in 1865.

****

It was a whirlwind journey through history, and Buddy was sure he had missed a lot. But it made an impression on him about the great accomplishments of the race. Maybe he would even follow-up some of what he heard by reading more about it. He didn't get bored! Sol was asked to take the discussion from there.

The Middle Passage

By the time this phase of the African Holocaust ended, tens of millions of African people (estimates are as high as 100,000,000) had been lost in the Middle Passage, murdered, raped, separated from family, language and religious group, beaten, forced into unpaid servitude, sold and handled like chattel, denied education in the ways of the New World, dehumanized and permanently stigmatized by color and racial identification as an inferior caste. Nevertheless, our enslaved Ancestors knew who we were, and articulated with stunning clarity, in English, what our new roles must be.

In *Ethiopian Manifesto* Robert Alexander Young states, "But learn, slaveholder, thine will rests not in your hand: God decrees to thy slave his rights as a man. This we issue forth as the spirit of the black man or Ethiopian's rights, established from the Ethiopian's Rock, the foundation of his civil and religious rights, which hereafter will be exemplified in the order of its course."[7]

David Walker, in his *Appeal To the Coloured Citizens of the World*, declares, "I promised in a preceding page to demonstrate to the satisfaction of the most incredulous, that we (coloured people of these United States of America), are the most wretched, degraded and abject set of beings that ever lived since the world began, and that white Americans having reduced us to the wretched state of slavery, treat us in that condition more cruel (they being an enlightened and Christian  people), than any heathen nation did any people whom it had reduced to our condition."[8] "I advance it therefore to you, not as a problematical, but as an unshaken and forever immovable fact, that your full glory and happiness, as well as all other coloured people under Heaven, shall never be consummated, but with the entire emancipation of your enslaved brethren all over the world."

Henry Highland Garnet's 1859 speech in Boston included these admonitions: "we, as colored people, had peculiar interests—

feelings and interests that no other people had—and that we understood the cause better than any others, and that if we wanted the work done at all we must do it ourselves; and that when we had accomplished the object, we should lay aside all distinctive labors, and come together as men and women, members of the great American family."[9]

Lack of clarity about identity was not evident in the public pronouncements of these Ancestors during slavery. By the turn of the century, we begin to see the contradictions and complexities of African people in America, emancipated without reparations or any claim to the land, besieged by Black Codes that were even more repressive than plantation protocols in most instances, terrorized by new white supremacist hate groups like the Ku Klux Klan, disenfranchised after a brief moment of democratic expression, and stymied by an inability to earn fair compensation for their skills and work products in the devastating wake of the defeat of Reconstruction.

"They shut it down hard," Herma sighed. "They even succeeded in translating a lot of their hatred and power-lust into law. The Black Codes totally restricted the movement, mobility, and liberty of the former slaves; and they took away the vote!" "They could not have done it without the help of the North," Sol responded. "They needed the raw goods from the South in order for the manufacturing industry of the North to rebound and flourish. Before long, it was back to business as usual—with Blacks virtually still enslaved, serving as sharecroppers and owing more than they earned to the 'company store' for goods purchased at jacked-up prices."

"Yes," Ra interjected, "but there were also self-help initiatives, mutual aid societies, and strong Black business start-ups. Many of our Ancestors turned that incredible devastation into their own opportunities—getting educated, owning homes, farms and banks, building businesses that employed and trained growing numbers of other Blacks. Helping one another with the mantra, 'Lift as you Climb!' It was an incredible time."

* * * * *

Further study: Genetic Memory

Ra asked Marguerite if she had found any more information about genetic memory and whether these experiences are embedded in the very DNA of African Americans even today. Marguerite reported that she had not found anything really definitive on genetic memory— theories are all over the place and are not at all conclusive. Yet, there do seem to be reasons to continue looking. Some postulate that our subconscious holds within it the experiences of persecution and degradation we historically experienced, individually and collectively—somehow imprinted on our current DNA. Some of the theories are linked to reincarnation and the belief that some of us actually were enslaved in a past life—which we remember on the subconscious level. On the other hand, some of the theories of reincarnation say that we come back as all different races and both genders over lifetimes—so everyone who is African American today did not have to have been Black in a prior life. "It's part of what are called Karmic debts and credits. I'll keep researching, and see what feels right to me," Marguerite concluded, "but, whatever the past or present influences are, we can and should focus on our ability to control our own thoughts and feelings, and bring only the positive into our lives." Everyone asked Marguerite to come back to these dynamics at other classes.

Buddy, in particular, wanted to hear more. All of this was new to him. If he could learn to control his thoughts and emotions—and especially his reactions to people and things in his life—he wanted to know how! Ra continued the historical and cultural thread at the next meeting.

Study Session Three

Ra said the definitive text on the realities, aspirations and learnings of the period right after the Civil War is W.E.B. Du Bois' *Souls of Black Folk*, published in 1903. It is in *Souls* that Dr. Du Bois prophesied, "The problem of the Twentieth Century is the problem of the color-line—the relation of the darker to the lighter races of men in Asia and Africa, in America and the islands of the sea."[10]

Du Bois and the fundamental dilemmas confronting African Americans

In the opening chapter, "Of Our Spiritual Strivings," Dr. Du Bois illuminates the fundamental dilemma that African Americans have always confronted: "It is a peculiar sensation, this double consciousness, this sense of always looking at one's self through the eyes of others, of measuring one's soul by the tape of a world that looks on in amused contempt and pity. One ever feels his two-ness—an American, a Negro; two souls, two thoughts, two unreconciled strivings; two warring ideals in one dark body, whose dogged strength alone keeps it from being torn asunder." (p.2) Du Bois continues: "This waste of double aims, this seeking to satisfy two unreconciled ideals, has wrought sad havoc with the courage and faith and deeds of ten thousand thousand people—has sent them often wooing false gods and invoking false means of salvation, and at times has even seemed about to make them ashamed of themselves." (p. 3)

> Such a double life, with double thoughts, double duties, and double social classes, must give rise to double words and double ideals, and tempt the mind to pretense or to revolt, to hypocrisy or to radicalism. In some such doubtful words and phrases can one perhaps most clearly picture the peculiar ethical paradox that faces the Negro of today and is tingeing and changing his religious life. Feeling that his rights and his dearest ideals are being trampled upon, that the public conscience is ever more deaf to his righteous appeal, and that all the reactionary forces of prejudice, greed, and revenge are daily gaining new strength and fresh allies, the Negro faces no enviable dilemma. Conscious of his impotence, and pessimistic, he often becomes bitter and vindictive; and his religion, instead of a worship, is a complaint and a curse, a wail rather than a hope, a sneer rather than a faith. On the other hand, another type of mind, shrewder and keener and more torturous too, sees in the very strength of the anti-Negro movement its patent weaknesses, and with Jesuitic casuistry is deterred by no ethical considerations in the endeavor to turn this weakness to the black man's strength. Thus we have two great and hardly reconcilable streams of thought and ethical strivings; the danger of one lies in anarchy, that of the other in hypocrisy. The one type of Negro stands

almost ready to curse God and die, and the other is too often found a traitor to right and a coward before force; the one is wedded to ideals remote, whimsical, perhaps impossible of realization; the other forgets that life is more than meat and the body more than raiment. (pp. 122-123)

Sol pointed out that each decade of the twentieth century and the first decade of the third millennium corroborated and supplied empirical evidence of the truth of Du Bois' definition of the identity crisis of African Americans. He asked: "To whom is Du Bois referring when he speaks of traitors, cowards, and hypocrites?" Names and faces flew through everyone's minds.

Members of this minority caste group have sought to escape its stigma and disrepute as individuals, to assimilate and become as much like the white majority as they possibly could, and have been rewarded in some instances—some more than others. Only when they are stopped by police for "driving while black," or when they are made the "fall guy" for policy gone awry, or when they slam their heads against the corporate "glass ceiling," or they are shown some comparable disrespect in whatever sphere they function—only then do they realize that they may appear to have made an individual escape, but they have not.

Herma jumped it here: Individuals want to "get paid," and they are paid for at least some period of time if they play the game acceptably; or, an individual might want publicity and fame, or to be chosen from the "shorter line." Some are willing to be actively and deliberately used to speak or work against the interests of their own people. For a few this will be possible, as long as the chosen exception represents the interests of the choosers well enough. You see this in the political arena every day. But, in reality, there can be no assimilationist individual escape; the question is: who is willing to deny the vast masses of our people, defile our Ancestors, and denounce our cultural mission in order to try?

Tom was a little uncomfortable. He said, "In order to live in the United States, or anywhere on this planet for that matter, accommodations must be made. The question is: where do we draw the line?"

Ra's response was, "This must be an explicit discussion we have, for which a contextual consensus answer is found, in the context of the African American cultural offensive. We will explore these questions and processes throughout our studies together.

"For example, why did Harry Belafonte say the nation's first African American Secretary of State, General Colin Powell, was acting like a house slave? What was behind Representative J.C. Watts' leaving the Congress and his leadership position in the Republican Party? Why do Representative Maxine Waters and other members of the Congressional Black Caucus publicly criticize their Democratic Party for taking the African American voter for granted, while depending upon the African American vote? After selling Black Entertainment Television to Viacom and remaining as CEO, did Bob Johnson, the first African American billionaire, oppose the cancellation of what he had called his favorite programs—the network's only public affairs programming—and fail to prevail? Why were we sharply divided in our opinions about whether Condoleezza Rice should be appointed the first African American woman Secretary of State? Should President Obama have sent official representatives of his Administration to the 2009 United Nations Conference that studied outcomes from the previous conference on Race, Racism, Xenophobia and Related Intolerance? Would Michael Jackson have been regarded the King of Pop globally if he had not whitened and altered his appearance? Were you in support of President Obama's nomination of Sonia Sotomayor for the Supreme Court? Is the Obama Administration doing enough to address the entrenched problems facing the African American community?"

You can cite many other such questions. Do so, and discuss them within your circles.

Tom continued: "Dr. Du Bois also spoke of individuals who seek to break out of the stigma of caste status by means of violent or radical resistance, holding to ideas and ideals that are impossible to realize. Anarchists without regard for law or custom; criminals who justify taking life and property as their payment for oppression; nihilists who have given up on finding or creating meaning and sink into putrefying hatred; abusive parents, clergy, or teachers who inflict their rage upon children, are examples of anti-social, anti-group, antagonists who fall within this category. They use the horrors and excesses of the white supremacy system to rationalize patterns of behavior and actions that are similarly horrific. Murder, rape, arson, theft, and the destabilization of families and communities have been committed and excused away in the name of a personal revolution. They hold us all back," Tom concluded bitterly.

"Here, again," Herma said, "the problem is that there can be no individual escape. Revolution by some specific definition may indeed be called for, but it must grow out of our cultural consensus and be organized and conducted by our group if it is to succeed as a moral imperative."

Sol asked, "In our history, who among the radicals helped to build an organized or institutional niche for our development and uplift, and who hurt our cause?

"Who was seeking personal wealth, fame or infamy, and who was building structures of resistance and group advancement?

"Who consistently pursued a vision of change, and who changed when other opportunities presented themselves?

Consider this question
"How do we, as a people, deliberate about nonviolent social change versus the perceived need for targeted violence; an inside-outside strategy versus never collaborating with the enemy; use of the media versus silence and secret plans; developing our own mega-businesses and multinational corporations; funding our own initiatives and compensating and evaluating our own workers versus depending upon outside money and standards?"

Buddy asked Aida to share some of her stories about these kinds of issues.

"The Black College campuses where I spent my childhood were villages within a larger small town and a cosmopolitan southern city," Aida began.

"Within the village, all the adults had the same expectations for all the children and for each other, and their values and expectations were moored by an accountability system. Most people saw each other every day, and the direct personal contact helped to maintain accountability. When there was slippage in the behavior of a child, all the adults who were directly involved asserted their prerogative to correct it: the teacher, the neighbor who heard about it while the child was on the way home, and of course the parents and grandparents. There was absolute consistency.

"The adults held one another accountable in many different ways, reflecting the complexity of the situations they were faced with. For example, my grandfather and the men in leadership on the campus used to play croquet every Sunday evening. He took me with him; and I remember the low hum of their voices as they planned the life of the college and of the town. They planned a boycott of the downtown shops as a response to the racism of the shopkeepers both in hiring and in their treatment of Negro customers. In the days without twitter, FaceBook, websites, Internet—and even word processing, they got the word out about the boycott by word of mouth through their college, their churches, lodges, clubs and every day movements throughout town. I went with my grandfather on his horse-drawn surrey to meet the country folks on the road on their way to town on Saturday to shop. He would explain to them that we were not buying so much as a spool of thread from the shops in town; he would take their orders and fill them from other places, bring the goods to them and settle up the monies with them. Because many of the farm workers knew my grandfather and some worked on his farm, they believed and trusted him. If anyone made his or her way into the shops anyway, or made it their business to try to go and tell the shopkeepers about the boycott in an effort to curry favor from them, one of the leaders was on the street to intercept them and turn them back. The one who persisted and, knowing the plan and scale of the effort, got to the white man in the effort to undermine his own people, would not be welcomed back into the circle and confidence of the Black community. It was the 1940's version of banishment. There is much to discuss when it comes to group accountability—many stories to tell," Aida concluded.

Ra said, "These are explicit issues to be addressed as the cultural offensive progresses. We should not just discuss them here in the safe space of our study group. At some point the MI team must take the discussion out to our homes, churches, associations, fraternities and sororities, lodges, clubs, colleges, online social networks, union halls, recreation areas, ball courts and fields, beauty and barber shops, and in our schools and after-school programs. What kind of discussion could we have about this on FaceBook? We must discuss and make decisions about these matters, together."

The team had lots of ideas and suggestions; and the discussion lasted a long, productive time.

Herma and Marguerite made their way over to Tom, to be sure he was all right. Herma thought he needed more experience with the way policy and politics are done. Marguerite thought he needed more faith. He was happy to know they cared enough about him to check in. However, his main questions were economic: how are we going to own the means of production and stop being exploited labor or merely consumers, all over the world? He was determined to find answers.

Buddy got up to help Aida with the food and dishes. His head was full of thoughts, questions, answers, and reactions to what he had heard; and he felt emotional in a strange, new way. He wanted to be near Aida. Maybe he would tell her what he was thinking and feeling when they got in the kitchen. Ra and Sol were planning the next class, the next move, the next level of MI work. They would need to talk with Aida too.

Four
VISION AND PURPOSE

"This the American black man knows: his fight here is a fight to the finish. Either he dies or wins. If he wins it will be by no subterfuge or evasion of amalgamation. He will enter modern civilization here in America a black man on terms of perfect and unlimited equality with any white man, or he will enter not at all. Either extermination root and branch, or absolute equality. There can be no compromise. This is the last great battle of the West."
—W.E.B. Du Bois, Black Reconstruction

Perfect and unlimited equality. African-descended people can bring into focus and share the vision of the perfect and unlimited equality of our group with any and all of the world's great groups, which is predicated upon the perfect and unlimited equality of each person to any other person. This sacred concept is an essential part of our historical intellectual and cultural legacy.

Focusing on a central concept is the heart of a "visioning process"— which is what this study is designed to engender. Think about the central concept of "perfect and unlimited equality"—individually and in your groups—and envision what you DO want, leaving aside for now all the challenges, barriers, and facets of what you do not want. Visioning focuses on the reality you DO want to bring into being.

Study Session Four

Ra started the next discussion by quickly recapping the myriad material contributions enslaved and free Africans have made to the building of the world's only superpower. He said, "Our knowledge and skill in agriculture, carpentry and masonry, among many other skills, literally built this nation. Over the decades, vast offerings in education, in the arts and entertainment, in science, health and technology, in business, and in mutual aid have also been made."

More fundamental and important than all of these, however, is a gift growing directly out of the soil of ancient Egyptian Maatian ethics, righteousness and justice.[1] It was the African and indigenous natives of North America who gave it the precious, sacred concept of democracy. Let's read again from Du Bois:

> It was the black man that raised a vision of democracy in America such as neither Americans nor Europeans conceived in the eighteenth century and such as they have not even accepted in the twentieth century; and yet a conception which every clear sighted man knows is true and inevitable. The white serfs, as they were transplanted in America, began a slow, but in the end effective agitation for recognition in American democracy. And through them, has risen the modern American labor movement. But this movement almost from the first looked for its triumph along the ancient paths of aristocracy and sought to raise the white servant and laborer on the backs of the black servant and slave. If now the black man had been inert, unintelligent, submissive, democracy would have continued to mean in America what it means so widely still in Europe, the admission of the powerful to participation in government and privilege in so far and only in so far as their power becomes irresistible. *It would not have meant a recognition of human beings as such and the giving of economic and social power to the powerless.* (Emphasis added.)

It is usually assumed in reading American history that whatever the Negro has done for America has been passive and unintelligent, that he accompanied the explorers as a beast of burden and accomplished whatever he did by sheer accident; that he labored because he was driven to labor and fought because he was made to fight. This is not true. On the contrary, it was the rise and growth among the slaves of a determination to be free and an active part of American democracy that forced American democracy continually to look into the depths; that held the faces of American thought to the inescapable fact that as long as there was a slave in America, America could not be a freed republic; and more than that: as long as there were people in America, slave or nominally free, who could not participate in government and industry and society as free, intelligent human beings, our democracy had failed its greatest mission.

One cannot think then of democracy in America or in the modern world without reference to the American Negro. The democracy established in America in the eighteenth century was not, and was not designed to be, a democracy of the masses of man and it was thus singularly easy for people to fail to see the incongruity of democracy and slavery. It was the Negro himself who forced the consideration of this incongruity, who made emancipation inevitable and made the modern world at least consider if not wholly accept the idea of a democracy including men of all races and colors.[2]

"This is really deep!" Herma affirmed. "I remember in my travels to England, how surprised I was to see so much class stratification—the great differences between the royals and the masses—families even making decisions about their choice of homes based upon what some member of the royal family wanted. They use even subtle ways the language is spoken to make distinctions as well. It may not still be in their laws, but it certainly is important in their customs and how they live every day. I couldn't believe it."

"I want us to consciously organize around our gift of democracy," Herma said. "We should be looking at this from every angle: democracy in the economy; democracy in the work place; democracy in international relations; democracy in the classroom; democracy in every part of society. What would our perfect equality mean in every case?"

Tom thought about what he had read about Europe and Asia, and he had to agree that something was different about the notions of equality found in African- descended people and Native Americans. He was trying to remember what he had read about the Iroquois belief system and how it had influenced the U.S. Constitution and Declaration of Independence.

Sol was pacing the floor. The importance of this—and the implications of this—were enormous for him. "No one thinks of us in this way," he began. "We don't even think of ourselves in this way! But if we can come to grips with what this means, we may find the handle we need for discussions about a cultural mission! Let me think this through. Help me!"

Spiritual Truths
Marguerite was thinking about the spiritual truths, and their emphasis on Oneness and our all being children of the Creator—all the explanation of equality she had ever seemed to need. So...put these truths into action—bring into being what we DO want! "I want us to realize the sacredness of our identity as African-descended people, so we can focus on our group development and organize around an agenda we can build together and agree upon," she said. Buddy was stunned; he had never read or heard anything like this. He had never thought African Americans had played such an amazing role. He felt a deep pang of pain when he recalled the raging emotion of boys his age when they felt disrespected, or betrayed—especially by one within their own small circle. If we are all equals, the worst thing you can do is disrespect me. There had been fighting. There had been violence with weapons. Friends had been lost forever. "I want us to understand why disrespecting each other is so painful and causes so much devastation, so we will stop the madness and start building each other up," Buddy whispered.

"Maybe this could become the handle for the cultural mission Sol was talking about. Maybe I can be a part of the discussion; and I can begin with my friends. I get this one," Buddy thought out loud.

The vision and expectation of perfect and unlimited equality for our group are explicit dimensions of our ethical identity. Let us see if we can agree upon this vision in the twenty-first century.

Five
CONNECTING THE DOTS

Buddy and Sol had talked a lot about democracy and equality since the last session, and they had planned an exercise for the group for the next gathering.

Study Session Five

Buddy started the exercise: "RESPECT! One way of saying we will not accept the dehumanization, disenfranchisement, and discrimination inflicted upon our people is to say we demand respect." Everyone applauded!

Sol took his turn: "Many African-descended young adults are ready and eager for cognitive, experiential and effective leadership with an explicit agenda to get our whole group the respect we deserve.

"Whether we are leaders in the academic, entertainment, professional, civil service, Hip Hop, private, entrepreneurial, athletic, artistic, religious or independent sectors, we are faced with the irony of being regarded by conventional wisdom as the least concerned about social uplift, when we regard ourselves as the most dissatisfied with the status quo including the established leadership.

"We are acutely aware that the vice of caste stigma has clamped down on all of us, but we see virtually no leadership, vision, or methodology for an effective, current and future, group response."
Buddy jumped back in: "We feel the disrespect, contempt and fear of society focused against us, but we did not create or permit our condition of being both the best and the least well educated, the most and the least privileged, the best connected and the most estranged cohort in the history of this group."

Herma joined in: "There is a bond among us that bridges the contradictions and heightens the ironies, but it is not uniformly conscious, intentional and goaloriented."

Sol started the group exercise:

Values

C🔴NNECT the D🔴TS

from us as 21st Century African American young adults back to ancient Kemet, where our Ancestors said, "If you are a leader and command many, strive for excellence in all you do so that no fault can be found in your character. For Maat (the way of Truth, Justice and Righteousness) is great; its value is lasting and it has remained unequalled and unchanged since the time of its Creator. It lies as a plain path before even the ignorant and those who violate its laws are punished."[1]

Truth

Everyone then joined in the exercise, adding categories as their interests directed them.

Pathfinders

CONNECT
the **DOTS**

from us as 21st Century African American young adults back to Robert Alexander Young, David Walker and Henry Highland Garnett, who, as enslaved Ancestors, affirmed that the Creator is the granter of equality, not men; and that, if the enslaved Africans were to uplift and advance, they must take responsibility for doing it themselves.

Waymakers

C⬤NNECT the D⬤TS

from 21st Century African American young adults back and to Harriet Tubman, who went back to rescue others from slavery with a pistol on her hip and who was reported to have told frightened fugitives who wanted to turn back and thereby jeopardize the safety of the others, "You will be free or die."

Innovators

C⬤NNECT the D⬤TS

from 21st Century African American young adults back to...our enslaved Ancestors who had been expert farmers, architects and builders for thousands of years when they were required to build the economy and the physical infrastructure of the United States of America from the ground up, while being treated like ignorant children.

Original Entrepreneurs

C**O**NNECT the D**O**TS

from us as 21st Century African American young adults back to Madame C.J. Walker and C. C. Spaulding, who built million-dollar businesses that served their people even in the devastation of the post-Reconstruction period and the Great Depression.

Educators

CONNECT the DOTS

from us as 21st Century African American young adults back to Mary McLeod Bethune, Booker T. Washington and the other pioneers who founded colleges and schools, and to their teachers, in order to bridge their people's knowledge divide from the Old World to the New, after centuries of forced illiteracy and ignorance.

Inventors

C●NNECT the D●TS

from us as 21st Century African American young adults back to George Washington Carver, Dr. Charles Drew, Elijah McCoy and all the other brilliant scientists who unlocked the secrets of nature to heal, and invented labor-saving devices to improve the quality of life of those who were poor, ill and ignored.

Law makers

from us as 21st Century African American young adults back to Charles Hamilton Houston, Thurgood Marshall, Constance Baker Motley and all of the attorneys who astutely and painstakingly built legal strategy over decades in order to dismantle the government-sanctioned system of racial segregation.

Spiritual Leaders

CONNECT the DOTS

from us as 21st Century African American young black adults to Adam Clayton Powell, Martin Luther King, Jr., Bishop Desmond Tutu and all the clergy who interpreted the Word as an undeniable call to justice in the lives of the oppressed and despised, and accepted the duty to put their faith into works, even at their own extreme peril.

Community Empowerers

C⬤NNECT
the D⬤TS

from us as 21st Century African American young adults back to Marcus Garvey, Fannie Lou Hamer, Daisy Bates, Ella Baker, Medgar Evers, Dorothy Height and Maulana Karenga, who used their considerable personal charisma to build institutions to advance the political and social agendas of their day.

Liberators

CONNECT the DOTS

from us as 21st Century African American young adults back to Nat Turner, Malcolm X, Stokely Carmichael (later Kwame Toure) and the other militant change-agents who understood the power dimension of the struggle and engaged the masses in the sojourn to liberty or death, "Black is Beautiful" and "Black Power".

Historic Visionaries

C⬤NNECT the D⬤TS

from us as 21st Century African American young adults back to Frederick Douglass' oral histories and autobiography, and the immaculate scholarly bodies of work of historians W.E.B. Du Bois, John Hope Franklin, and Sterling Stuckey.

Truth Speakers

from us as 21st Century African American young adults back to Phillis Wheatley, Zora Neale Hurston, Langston Hughes, Sterling Brown, James Baldwin, Nikki Giovanni, The Last Poets, Gil Scott Heron and all the poets, writers and storytellers who affirmed the truth and plumbed the depths of our human experience through the spoken and written word.

Musicians

CONNECT the DOTS

from us as 21st Century African American young adults back to the unforgettable musicians of protest, resistance and rage, Paul Robeson, Billie Holliday, Miles Davis, Odetta, Nina Simone, and Sweet Honey in the Rock; and even back to the enslaved ancestors who made the violin talk when their drums were outlawed and whose Spirituals gave birth to the blues, gospel, jazz, R&B, and Hip Hop—the only authentic American music, the irresistible creative proof of our humanity and our value.

Filmmakers

CONNECT the DOTS

from us as 21st Century African American young adults back to stereotype-smashing, image-uplifting filmmakers, Euzhan Palcy Melvin Van Peebles, Haile Gerima, Ousmane Sembene, Julie Dash, who set new standards for truth-telling.

Social Change Makers

CONNECT the DOTS

from us as 21st Century African American young adults back to the social analysts who illuminated the nature of our complex relationship to ourselves, Franz Fanon, E. Franklin Frazier, and Carter G. Woodson.

Seekers of Physical Excellence

from us as 21st Century African American young adults back to the physical and spiritual specimens who survived the Middle Passage and became the most extraordinary athletes on the planet, systematically transforming every organized sport they were able to play, and uniquely creating unparalleled dance, sport and endurance regimens.

Communicators

from us as 21st Century African American young adults back to journalists William Monroe Trotter, Ida B. Wells Barnett, Robert Abbot, and Hoyt Fuller whose mighty crusades against racism, lynching and discrimination and for defining our own cultural aesthetic, ideals and goals redefined our place in current events.

Nurturers

from us as 21st Century African American young adults back to the Institution builders Haki R. Madhubuti, Safisha Madhubuti, and Barbara A. Sizemore; and to the parents who loved, nurtured and taught their children—brought them up to be a credit to themselves, their families and their race— even in the degradation of enslavement, sharecropping, unemployment, terrorism, disenfranchisement and public ridicule.

Defining our future

The study group session ended amid cheers, laughing, applause, and high fives, especially with Buddy. Marguerite was sure the Ancestors had come to join them; she felt their presence strongly and she was so grateful. Sol asked Buddy if he enjoyed the session, and if he was proud of his contribution. Buddy said he was totally boosted. He saw Aida beaming at him. What a session!

Six

SELF-KNOWLEDGE, SELF-LOVE

Study Session Six

At the next study group session, Sol asked Ra if he could open the discussion that followed their Connect the Dots session. He had a particular reason. He said:

If we can connect the dots, we can achieve three vitally important objectives: we can rekindle the hot flames of self-knowledge and self love; we can harness and channel the enormous energies of our people into a sense of collective purpose; and we can finally answer, with one voice, the most important question children can ask of their culture— "What difference does it make whether I live or die?" He did not look at Buddy, but he knew his younger brother was intensely self-conscious at that moment.

Self-knowledge is the key that unlocks each of our unique, infinite, spiritual, mental, emotional and physical powers. It is hard to say what could be more important! When you don't know who you are, whose you are, what you are connected to, what your people have believed and accomplished, and what you should be doing based upon these facts, you are lost.

We've come this far
The terror, anguish and utter disorientation experienced by the African people who were enslaved are unimaginable and unspeakable. The enslavers' methods of divide and conquer, of separating families and keeping people who shared the same language or religion apart even in the holds of slave ships; of selling and threatening to sell children away from their mothers and husbands from their wives;

of rewarding house slaves and overseers while punishing field slaves and those whose resistance came to their attention, are well known. Enslavement in the United States was different from any other slavery known to man, though enslaving those defeated in war has been a common practice in all societies back to antiquity. The enslavement of our ancestors was called the "peculiar institution" because it branded African-descended people with the stigma of inferiority in perpetuity, based upon the color of their skin. In every other system of slavery, the enslaved could restore their humanity and status after fulfilling their forced obligation—but not the African and her and his descendants. The rape and concubinage forced upon many women, resulting in the birth of mulatto children, also served to inject the wedges of unequal treatment, color consciousness, and European standards of beauty.

Education in the language and of the ways of the New World was explicitly prohibited. The condition of being owned, violated, beaten, chained, worked mercilessly, sustained only marginally in terms of basic necessities such as food, shelter and clothing, and denied any modicum of control over one's life was viciously cruel. Being forced to demonstrate, verbally and nonverbally, the triumph of European brain over African brawn was intensely oppressive.

Every device to dehumanize, isolate, intimidate and confound the African was used, to erase his and her identity as a free and accomplished equal, and to force an acceptance of permanent caste degradation.

Great destruction did indeed occur; however the long African memory was not completely obliterated.[1] Consider this statement:

> ...the Southern slave, ever forming the creative, radiating center of the black ethos in America, through his music and dance, through his folktales and religion, projected much that was African into an essentially European environment. In the North, the fact that almost all blacks, as late as the second decade of the Nineteenth Century, referred to themselves as either "Africans" or "free Africans" demonstrates that they marked themselves off — and were marked off by force of circumstances — from the larger society. There is

little evidence that, for blacks generally, being American was considered desirable, even if attainable, until well into the Nineteenth Century. What, then, was the sense of reality out of which the ideology of Black Nationalism was fashioned? A consciousness of a shared experience of oppression at the hands of white people, an awareness of group traits and preferences in spite of a violently anti-African larger society, a recognition of bonds and obligations between Africans everywhere, an irreducible conviction that Africans in America must take responsibility for liberating themselves-these were among the pivotal components of the world view of the black men who finally framed the ideology.

With a deep dedication to African peoples at the center of their consciousness, with the contradiction between American practice and preachment starkly evident in the post "Revolutionary" period, two black men, Robert Alexander Young and David Walker, speculated on the status of African peoples in a way which broke beyond the shackles which America sought to impose on the African mind. They created black nationalist ideology. [Young's Ethiopian Manifesto and Walker's Appeal to the Colored Citizens of the World were published in 1829]. (pp.S-7)

So, I ask you—and I would like for everyone to answer in his and her own way:

Who are we?
Ra took this one: We have already addressed this issue in a number of ways, but it is so important that we are clear. We are the parents of all humanity. We are spiritual, creative definers and builders of an ancient culture whose most prominent feature is a regard and respect for "human beings as such." This culture has been devastated by 500 years of enslavement, degradation and discrimination, but it has not been destroyed. We are now called to engage in cultural renewal, together, to build upon the best of our legacy, to correct faults and flaws, and to once again become the Village our Ancestors envisioned and created for us.

Whose are we?
Marguerite was anxious to answer: We belong to our Creator, our Ancestors, to each other, and to our children, born and unborn. We are not African-descended people by accident - there is a divine purpose and plan for our life together, as well as for our individual lives. We share our wonderful talents, perspectives and productivity with the world.

What are we connected to?
Herma saw the connection to public policy: Our ancient African village[2] where a strong cultural infrastructure was in place and the roles and functions of members of our society were well ordered and scrupulously observed, is today but a romantic metaphor. It is impossible to say how the old structures would have changed and adapted to new global realities, had they been unencumbered by colonialism and the forced exodus of so many millions of their members.

***

Ra became more emphatic: It is difficult, but, I maintain, it is not impossible for our group to define and implement new structures and patterns making for a higher quality of life, in keeping with our most fundamental cultural values. We do still, somehow, have qualities, characteristics and behaviors that are distinctively ours, as demonstrated by the excellence we have achieved in the areas in which we have been able to function, by our political and spiritual profiles, by our consumer habits, and by our extended family ties and bond with the elders and Ancestors.

Aida observed that, unlike her Black College village of the 1940s and 50s, in the 21st century our village will not be small, it will not be located in one place specific, and membership in it will not be mandatory. We are connected to each other through our kinship and cultural bonds. Our village will exist in the minds and hearts of those of us who choose to exalt in these bonds, in time and space—in many places, and by means of the technology and communications devices that are and will be available in the third millennium. And how will this choice be made? What will compel individuals, families, groups, neighborhoods, cyber groupings, and voluntary self-conscious cultural enclaves around the globe to form themselves? If the negative aspects of our shared reality are not enough to compel us to choose group identity and group advancement—what positive aspects of our journey through time, right now, and into the future can we develop a better understanding of and message about? What kind of strategic communications will enable us to build the cultural infrastructure we so desperately need? I can hug you and celebrate your success if you are right here with me. I can give you "the eye" when you misbehave, when you are within eyeshot. As a group, we can praise you when you exemplify our values, and castigate you when you betray our principles to your face, and also by the way we support or shun you in public or electronic contexts beyond the confines of our group. What are our effective rewards and punishments?

A central element in the building of a cultural infrastructure is the wholehearted agreement of the adults of the group, in certain commonly-held expectations for behavior and accountability. We must state what we believe in, what we reward, and what we punish; and then we must live up to our statement. This is a critical component of the work we must do together, in order to become that village.[3]

What have our people believed?
Marguerite looked first at Aida, then offered: We have believed in a Higher Power than ourselves at least from the earliest written records of our sojourn on this planet, going back to the Nile Valley civilizations. Praise, gratitude, inspired wisdom, protection, and the acceptance of personal and group responsibility to live in accordance with sacred principles have characterized our relationship to the Creator.

We have believed that our Ancestors, on whose shoulders we stand and because of whose excellence and sacrifice we are where we are today, remain a force in our lives. They have been way showers, by whose example our path in the current time can be illuminated. They have given us the gifts of life and advancement, and we owe them a great debt which we must endeavor in every way to repay. Central to our obligation to the Ancestors is the charge to sustain, improve, and pass on our culture to succeeding generations, and to envision a future of selfdetermination and prosperity.

We believe that the divine gift of life is sacred within each person, and that this gift confers equality among human beings—and the demand for democracy. It is not physical attributes, talents, privileges or opportunities that define the parameters of equality, it is the fact of the Creator's gift of human life: all who have that great gift are equals.

As equals, we should be free, then, as individuals and as a group, to be selfdetermining within our culture and to engage fully in the larger society, even when we live in nations other than our own. We value human life over property or objects; and the sanctity of personal one-on-one relationships must be respected.[4]

> Always there was this moral commitment, born of the slavery and Reconstruction experience that united most members of the community in pursuing common goals: respect as human beings, unfettered participation in the economic and political life of this country, full civil liberties and equal protection under the law. (Marable, op. cit., p.l8)

What have our people accomplished?
Herma was first to respond: In addition to material accomplishments and the vast and deep cultural infrastructure our people have brought into being, it is critically important that we understand that African people were the first to define what it means to form a society, to establish the state, to govern peaceful and prosperous nations. Nile Valley societies (the first for which we have written records) were centers of good governance, learning, commerce, beauty, artistic and architectural accomplishment—and are the foundation for the best in the Greek and succeeding European societies that followed. *What should we be doing in light of these facts?*

Tom was ready to participate: We must become explicitly group-conscious, develop a shared vision for the 21st century together, organize like we have never organized before—in order to implement and institutionalize that vision, and authentically improve the quality of life of African-descended people all around the planet.

We must focus upon what we do want, rather than what we do not want. We must develop the will to be united, rather than divided. We must insist that the condition of African-descended people must improve—and that we ourselves must take responsibility for improving it, becoming owners and builders and not just laborers and consumers. We must plant the seed of righteousness, confidence, and faith that we have the power to effect authentic change, and then nurture and grow that seed with the help of the Creator and the Ancestors, each other, and all fair-minded people of good will.

Ra pointed out that the Mission Inevitable team had chosen its mission for these very reasons, these very answers to the Question. He said, "A critical mass of us must accept leadership, begin to engage in a consensus-building process, arrive at some statements of principle, articulate some immediate, medium- and long-term goals, and conduct a world-class campaign to win the hearts and minds of our people. It is reasonable, and, in fact, compelling to acknowledge that we must arrive at a group agenda and see it through! There are many agendas already in some form- start with these and shape the one we can agree to implement. We must prevail!"

As Dr. Du Bois told us,

> I tried to say to the American Negro: during the time of this frontal attack which you are making upon American and European prejudice, and with your unwavering statement and restatement of what is right and just, not only for us, but in the long run, for all men; during that time, there are certain things you must do for your own survival and self-preservation. You must work together in unison; you must evolve and support your own social institutions; you must transform your attack from the foray of an organized body. (Du Bois, Color and Democracy: Colonies and Peace (NY: Harcourt, Brace, 1945, pp.l12-3)

Self-love

Sol took this one, looking directly at Buddy as he responded: Self-hatred is at the root of many dysfunctions within African-descended individuals, families, and communities. Its opposite, self-love, is the root of spiritual, emotional, mental and even physical well-being. Self-loving individuals bring stability, sanity and a sense of the sacred to their families and communities. The prerequisite to self-love is self knowledge.

When African-descended people have a clear understanding of who we are in the sweep of human history, and when we engage together in cultural analysis for the purpose of renewing the vehicle that will move our group forward, love for self and family and group is inspired.

Aida responded to Sol's long stare in her direction by saying, "I remember well a period of our history, in the 1950s and 60s, when our Movement galvanized the energies and passions of a critical mass of African Americans, filling us to overflowing with self love. Our effectiveness in organizing was matched only by our genuine regard for one another, across class lines. Our dedication displaced most forms of juvenile delinquency and street crime. Fresh currents of vigorous intellectual and creative work flowed through our endeavors. Our desire to affirm and create a better future for ourselves together was stronger than any competing interests— and it can be again—this time with an economic dimension that matches the social and political gains that have been won. It is still so strong and fresh for me, in heart and mind. It is the reason I care so much for you, and form the study groups that will help you attain self-knowledge and self-love, leading to action for our group advancement."

Sense of purpose
Ra took this one: A recognition of the essential characteristic of our ethical identity as a people gives us a great and compelling sense of purpose. If we are meant to teach humanity the meaning of democracy, and to insist that each and every life on earth is sacred and must be treated equally, then our work is noble and vast, and there is much yet to be done, all over the planet—including our own communities, globally.

If planting and cultivating seeds of true democracy is our collective vocation, then we can see the organizing principle of all our historic achievements in this light- and we can chart a future course together accordingly. Let's do it!

Answer the children's Question. The answer to the heart-stopping Question of an African-descended child, "What difference does it make whether I live or die?" is clear and compelling. How should we answer? To Sol's gratified surprise, Buddy, who had been meeting on his own with Aida, stood up and said:

> Dear Ones,
>   *You are the next in line of a great ancient people whose work on this planet is not done. We need you, to fulfill both your individual purpose and your part in our group purpose. You are absolutely essential to our success. The Creator has endowed us with everything we need in order to fulfill our purpose; and our Ancestors remain with us to guide our steps and blaze the light of truth upon our path. We want you to know yourself and to love yourself, the way we know and love you. We will cherish you, teach you, protect you, and join with you as we renew our culture and uplift our race together. We will lead you, and follow you, as we redeem our vitally important collective vocation on this planet. We must follow you as you look into the future and dream dreams we cannot even imagine! Let me talk with you, and listen to your views, about our purpose. Together, we will draw a blueprint to make our lives better and to improve the world. Let's begin right now.*

Aida hugged Buddy, looked at him, and said to the group, "Particular qualities, talents and gifts of each child should then be identified, articulated, explained, praised, and discussed with the young person. Ideas and plans, dreams and visions about how each child's unique purpose can be realized should begin. Ongoing support and guidance from at least one caring adult must be assured. Every African-descended adult should give his or her rendition of this answer to every African-descended child when this Question is asked or implied, and then be sure every aspect of the response is realized." Still hugging and praising Buddy, they ended the session.

Seven
WHAT CAN WE DO?

Study Session Seven

Ra began the next session: "It is one thing to set an agenda for our people that speaks to what other folks should do with and for us; and it is, of course, extremely important that we state what we expect from the US government, from state and local government, and from the private sector.[1] However, for our purposes in MI, let us focus on an agenda that spells out what WE will do. An agenda that we set for ourselves, and agree to, is one we will control and be accountable for."

"Maulana Karenga has given us the annual cultural celebration of Kwanzaa. Its seven principles, the Nguzo Saba, are Unity (Umoja), Self-determination (Kujichagulia), Collective Work and Responsibility (Ujima), Cooperative Economics (Ujamaa), Purpose (Nia), Creativity (Kuumba), and Faith (Imani)."

Principles for life

Herma was adamant when she asked: "Can we extend the network of Africandescended young adults who subscribe to these seven principles and make the personal and family commitment to live by them? Not just in the week between Christmas and New Year's, but all year long, each day, the seven principles can be a guide to group-conscious living. Can you cite examples of daily practices that would make the Nguzo Saba habits of thought and behavior in your heart, your home and your community? Do certain authors or artists come to mind when you think of each principle? Does your home library include children's books that exemplify the principles; what about your music, video and film libraries?"

Marguerite asked to be recognized and said: "The key is to form good habits. Habits embed themselves in our subconscious; we perform according to our habits without consciously thinking. Perhaps the greatest gift the Creator has given us is the ability to control our thoughts and feelings. These thoughts and feelings become our habits."

"When we train ourselves to live according to affirmative cultural principles such as the Nguzo Saba, we develop a habitual positive spirit of uplift and advancement for ourselves and our people. Good habits can also dissolve and replace bad habits, including addictions. We can consciously form good habits by focusing on their importance to us, repeating and affirming them in our minds, and recognizing and removing thoughts that are counter to the positive habits we want to instill. Think of it as weeding your garden, and planting the produce and flowers you want, rather than letting the weeds overtake the garden. This is a life-long process; but we see immediate results when we begin to monitor and correct our thoughts and feelings, and gift ourselves with this wonderful habit."

Sol asked, not just looking at Buddy, but at each MI team member: "Have you ever thought about what you think? Follow your thoughts, particularly when your mind is still or idle—what do your thoughts go to? Are they constructive and helpful, or destructive and harmful? Remember that we must control our thoughts and feelings, not the other way around. When you find that your habits of thought are not positive or do not strengthen your cultural will, you can change them simply (though not immediately, it takes some time) by dismissing or releasing what you do not want and replacing it with what you do want."

Taking control of our personal lives is the first step in building strong families and communities.

Ra picked up the thread: "Taking control of our personal lives is the first step in building strong families and communities. The first step in taking control of our personal lives is the conscious act of monitoring our every thought and feeling and aligning each of them with our highest spiritual and cultural intentions and affirmations. This is a powerful place to start our processes of cultural renewal. Beginning with personal growth, self mastery, and group thinking, we till and feed the soil that will become fertile for our harvest."

With your loved ones, and in your groups, social online networks, and other close associations, talk about these processes. Support one another in reflection, study and arriving at new understandings. Support one another in putting behind us old negative, destructive vestiges of self- and group hatred. Look together at specific instances when counterproductive decisions or activities occurred for lack of a positive cultural perspective. Lift up those times when good results were achieved because a clear and constructive cultural approach was taken.

Herma excitedly pointed out: "These principles move us from the personal realm into the societal realm. Can we extend the network of African-descended young adults who subscribe to the seven principles and make the personal and family commitment to live by them? Maybe we can ask everyone, what are your particular examples of how the principles can be used in everyday life? Think about and discuss their applications in personal life; in group life such as associations, clubs, fraternities and sororities and lodges; at work; at school; in faith-based settings; on FaceBook, and wherever you discuss current events in the United States and in other places around the world."

Ra agreed and said: "As we well know, study groups are a highly effective mechanism for this kind of inquiry. Forming study groups—by subject area, by age-group cohorts, by action outcome, or other groupings—will greatly enhance our cultural work in communities around the nation and around the world. Without cost, groups can meet in homes, online, or in libraries at regularly scheduled times, to study and discuss topics selected by the members of the group. Study groups may choose to focus on issues of identity and history, or on immediate situations within the community that need to be addressed, or on matters of ongoing concern such as the education of our children. Book clubs, bowling leagues, youth clubs, church circles, bridge and other parties, civic associations, and many other existing groups can devote some of their sessions to cultural study and discussion." (See Appendix 1: the bibliography is a place to begin organizing study group sessions.)

The beneficial effects of our engaging in study groups in large numbers will ramify out far beyond the immediate projects we take up—exponentially. "Make it viral!" This can be where our authentic uplift and advancement originates.

Aida was asked how this sounded to her, and she replied, "Forming study groups is easy when a group already seeks the knowledge; but when people are not group-conscious or organized for the purpose of advancing the race, we found it helpful to start with a powerful vision or goal, and invite them to share it with us and do something concrete to achieve it. Changing unjust laws that discriminated against us was straightforward and compelling, once we had Leaders with a plan as to how it could be done. Even after we were able to change the Jim Crow laws, there were targets like establishing African American Studies majors in colleges; preventing discrimination in admissions and hiring by way of affirmative action; and putting aggressive voter education and mobilization drives in place. You will want a critical mass of our people to share your vision for becoming a village again. When they do, they will see the value of adhering to group principles and sacrificing to attain self-mastery."

Sol saw the wisdom of Aida's advice. He reaffirmed the vision of the IM was to spearhead a major effort to get a critical mass of our people to share the vision of becoming our village again in the 21st century. Within IM he asked: Can *we* agree to honor, study and pass along the teachings of our Ancestors?

- Respect and care for our elders
- Protect, love, educate, spend time with and talk to, and hold the highest expectations for, each and every one of our children- every child must have at least one caring and responsible adult actively molding his or her life
- Be and remain advocates for our children in schools we carefully choose, throughout the years of their formal education
- Honor our families with faithfulness, healthy lifestyles, conflict resolution, financial, and moral support
- Reflect, study, deliberate, decide upon and agree to definitions and
- standards of righteous living to which we will hold one another accountable
- Behave righteously at home and in the community, with integrity and honesty, in accordance with the agreed-upon values of our culture and spiritual teachings
- Become ownership-minded; support our own businesses and turn each dollar over in our own communities at least four times,

making a serious commitment to asset- and wealth-building

- Engage in, and accept leadership for, the civic life of our communities, our nation, and the global village as culturally-inspired African-descended people

Dialogue of the most probing, honest and constructive sort is urgently needed among African Americans, in order to begin a serious process of arriving at collective, group conscious accountability systems.

Herma brought up the subject of reparations: Whatever the members of the U.S. House of Representatives do about moving John Conyers' bill HR40, to study slavery, its continuing effects and whether reparations are due to the descendants of slaves to a vote, we in the African American community, and the African world globally, must address these issues. We must address them together, arrive at certain conclusions, develop goals and strategies to achieve them, set time-tables for the implementation of a long-range plan of development and uplift, and carry out the plans.

Construct a blueprint for group uplift and advancement

Tom added: "We must construct a blueprint for group uplift and advancement, based upon our ancient cultural values and the best understanding we can have of the 21st century and the global economy. We have not paid enough attention to the economic dimensions of our condition. Obviously, the old, the young, the men, the women, the members of this or that political party, cannot do this alone. African Americans from all walks of life, from all regions of the country, from large cities, small towns, rural farmlands, and suburbs must put our heads and hearts together (even if virtually) to develop such a blueprint. We must place that blueprint in its global context, because it will have implications for African-descended people throughout the world. We live in a global economy and we should begin to act like it!"

Ra concurred and said, "A critical mass of those dedicated to the perfection of the African model for human expression must continue to solidify our approach to group life—because this work has already begun. In fact, in the 500 years of our holocaust, it has never stopped."

Marguerite quietly noted: "The Ancestors often had clear notions of what was needed."

"If we form a distinct class, and our present condition is not as we would wish it, and the betterment of that condition becomes a work of our own, what then shall we do for its accomplishment? It is well known and fully appreciated by many, that the general diffusion of useful knowledge is the great means of our moral elevation. And that the school, the pulpit, and the press are the natural and proper channels through which to communicate this knowledge, is also known."

To further illustrate my point, I paraphrase an Editorial from 1937: "If the school, the pulpit, and the press be the natural and legitimate means of our moral elevation, and that elevation, to be effectual, must be general, how shall these be brought to bear upon every individual of our race in the land? The answer: by ORGANIZED and systematic effort. Every youth should be educated; every minister should be a fountain of light; and a copy of the "Colored American" should be put into the hands of every family. To accomplish these, or either of them, requires organization and the concentration of our whole moral and pecuniary power.... All that is requisite to effect it, is the will."[2]

Tom marked issues of building unity: "The will to affect our own plans for betterment is a tragic casualty of the holocaust we have faced. It is now ever more difficult to bring consensus out of the many and varied choices we have, to spell out and agree to principles of correctness, to trim our personal indulgences in order to be accountable to the group. We have, in a sense, been trained to go against our own interests and to do the other man's work for him, to our own detriment. We have not had accountability systems in place to reward enough of our good businesses with strong profits, or to punish sell-outs, mercenaries and traitors with bankruptcy. We whine about how many times the dollar turns over in the other man's community and how few times in ours—but selective buying, boycotts, and doing business with our own are too often episodic. We have not made these decisions about accountability in this current time period. Nevertheless, this is precisely what we must do."

A final Word: We must engage in Cultural Revolution!
Ra became pointed and explicit: "We must engage with each other, behind closed doors, in a cultural revolution."

Cultural revolution means...the ideological and practical struggle to transform persons and people and to build structures to insure, maintain and expand that transformation. Cultural revolution...can be defined as the ideological and practical struggle to: (1) transform the cultural context in which people live; (2) transform them in the process, making them self-conscious agents of their own liberation; and (3) build the institutional base to sustain and constantly expand that transformation. It implies and necessitates revitalizing, creating and recreating culture." (Karenga, *op. cit.*, p.278 - 9)

Everyone sat in pensive silence. No one was in a rush to leave; but no one could put his or her thoughts into words at that moment either— or wanted to. It was a time of quiet reflection. Buddy was thinking, "I didn't know any one talked about revolution any more! I wonder what that means."

Eight
ACHIEVING OUR COLLECTIVE GREATNESS NOW

Ra got right to the point to begin the next session: "What would it mean for us to operationalize Maulana Karenga's definition of cultural revolution? That is, what would it take for us to transform the cultural context in which we live? What would it take for us to transform ourselves in the process, making ourselves self-conscious agents of our own liberation; and to then build the institutional base to sustain and constantly expand that transformation? Our blueprint for attaining perfect and unlimited equality for our group can begin here. Let's walk through it."

Study Session Eight
What is the cultural context in which we live in the 21st century?

Tom offered his thoughts first: "Unlike our Ancestors, African-descended people do not face (literal and widespread) enslavement, colonialism and black codes today; however, like our Ancestors, the cultural context imposed around the world by the United States and Western Europe is that of white supremacy, economic and political hegemony, and entrenched privilege for Whites at the expense of people of color in the new dimensions of globalization.[1]

We learn from Melvin Oliver and Thomas Shapiro, in *Black Wealth/White Wealth*, that, for example:

> The homestead laws that opened up the East during colonial times and West during the nineteenth century created vastly different opportunities for black and white settlers. One commentator even suggests land grants "allowed three-fourths of America's colonial families to own their own farms." Black settlers in California...found that their claims for home stead

status were not legally enforceable. Thus African Americans were largely barred from taking advantage of the nineteenth-century federal land-grant program. (p. 38)

A centerpiece of New Deal social legislation and a cornerstone of the modern welfare state, the old-age insurance program of the Social Security Act of 1935 virtually excluded African Americans and Latinos, for it exempted agricultural and domestic workers from coverage and marginalized low-wage workers....men's benefits were tied to wages, military service, and unionism rather than to need or any notion of equality. Thus blacks were disadvantaged in New Deal legislation because they were historically less well paid, less fully employed, disproportionately ineligible for military service, and less fully unionized than white men. In 1935...42 percent of black workers in occupations covered by social insurance did not earn enough to qualify for benefits compared to 22 percent for whites.

...the development of low-interest, long-term mortgages backed by the federal government marked the appearance of a crucial opportunity for the average American family to generate a wealth stake. The purchase of a home has now become the primary mechanism for generating wealth. However, the FHA's conscious decision to channel loans away from the central city and to the suburbs has had a powerful effect on the creation of segregated housing in post-World War II America.

The FHA's official handbook even went so far as to provide a model "restrictive covenant" that would pass court scrutiny to prospective white homebuyers. (p.40)

Restrictive covenants and other "segregation makers" have been ruled unconstitutional in a number of important court cases. But the legacy of the FHA's contribution to racial residential segregation lives on in the inability of blacks to incorporate themselves into integrated neighborhoods in which the equity and demand for their homes is maintained. This is seen most clearly in the fact that black middle-class homeowners end up with less valuable homes even when their incomes are similar to those of whites. (p. 39)

The impact of race and class are also channeled through institutional mechanisms that help to destabilize black communities. Insurance redlining begins to make it difficult and/ or expensive for homes and businesses to secure coverage. City services begin to decline, contributing to blight. As the community declines, it becomes the center for antisocial activities: drug dealing, hanging out, and robbery and violence. In this context the initial investment that the middle-class black family makes either stops growing and grows at a rate that is substantially lower than the rate at which a comparable investment made by a similarly well-off, middle-class white in an all-white community would gain in value. Racialized state policy contributed to this pattern, and the pattern continues unabated today. (p. 41)

More current analysis can be found in Reversal of Fortune Economic gains of 1990s overturned for African Americans from 2000-07 by Algernon Austin, among other articles and books.

How can we transform the cultural context in which we live in the 21st century into one that supports, nurtures and catalyzes our vision and goal of perfect and unlimited equality for our group?

Ra relished this one: "We will liberate ourselves from the cage of caste stigma only when we give reality to the power and promise of our own cultural renewal. We will force the truth of who we are upon the enemies of our truth only when we embrace, operationalize, and live that truth every day. We will change the material conditions of our lives when we change the spiritual and cultural conditions of our lives through group-conscious action. This is why I say, and I repeat, we will never sit at the table of the cultures of the world as equals unless and until we examine, correct where needed, and renew our cultural integrity and life."[2]

What can happen within each of us, and within our close personal groups, as we are transforming our cultural context and how will we know that we are self conscious agents of our own liberation?

Buddy listened intently as Marguerite responded first to this one: "The metamorphosis into self- and group-loving cultural worker is a journey from confusion to clarity, from indifference to passionate engagement, from estrangement or isolation to profound belonging. Lives that have been characterized by boredom become engaged lives. Lives that have been characterized by disillusionment become inspired lives. Close personal groups that have confined their interactions to people their own age, or class, political or religious groups, or nations of origin, find common cause and purpose with people from the other subgroups and ethnicities of our race, and with people of good will from all the world's great groups. Days that have been unfulfilling become days of enthusiasm and commitment. Months that have passed with no notable accomplishment become months during which one loses oneself in planning and working together to accomplish the group's great goal."

Sol joined in: "We will know we are self-conscious agents of our own liberation when individuals replace low self-esteem with deep confidence, insecurity with certainty, and ignorance and self-hatred with knowledge and self-love. When families mend broken relationships, tend to each other's wounds and re-establish the all-important bonds among men, women and children within families. When families embrace and live by our cultural principles and ethical standards. When communities systematically define, create, implement and monitor the cultural and institutional infrastructures that are needed to improve the quality of life of their members. When there is a robust e-communications system among African descended people globally to address and conduct policy and advocacy analysis, business development, social interventions and campaigns, and to enjoy our unmatched artistic expression."

The session ended with a lively discussion of the points that had been made. MI team members started to think in terms of actual plans they could put in place in their families and in the community. "Now we are moving into action!" Ra said as they adjourned.

Study Session Nine

To open the next study group session, Ra said: "Think about the institutions that make up society and its culture: the family, education, governance, faith and worship, systems of commerce, wealth-building and employment, law and justice, health, recreation, the arts and entertainment, defense, nonprofit organizations (non-governmental organizations, or civil society), and the media. What can and should we be doing for ourselves and with each other in these areas that have been found to be essential to the effective and efficient functioning of society? How can we be sure society's institutions are always helping us to achieve our goals; and what must we do when they are not? We can control more of this matrix than we may think we can."

Tom noted dryly: "There is an African-descended person doing everything anyone on this planet is doing. We just are not doing it for ourselves, together. This must change!"

The family is the most important unit of any society or culture.
Sol started the discourse on institutions, looking at Buddy: "The family is the most important unit of any society or culture. Survival of the group depends upon procreation, and this is the core, biological definition of family: descendants of a common ancestor. Families provide for the basic necessities of their members including food, shelter, clothing, love and protection.[3] Moreover, it is within the family unit, first and foremost, that the beliefs, values and behaviors appropriate to the culture of the group are passed on."[4]

Herma was convincing as she observed that: "Clearly, our blueprint for Achieving Our Collective Greatness Now must begin with plans to build, rebuild, nurture, strengthen, sustain and protect extended family units. Parents and their children must always have the advantage of being positioned within a network of their mothers, fathers, brothers, sisters, grandparents, aunts, uncles, cousins, friends and neighbors. If, for any reason whatsoever, parents are not able to perform the vital functions the family must perform, then we as cultural family must step in and help them."

"Individuals within each family must accept the responsibility to be disciplined and accountable to the beliefs, values and behaviors appropriate to the culture that are agreed-upon. The foundation of the culture is the family. Family with a cracked and broken foundation will have a structure that is deficient in serious ways; while family with a strong foundation will have the cultural infrastructure that can become vast, impermeable and everlasting."[5]

Focus on Education
Ra continued down the list: "Education, formal and informal, is the key to personal mastery and the group's ability to formulate a shared vision and plan its implementation. Education does not create personal or group advancement by itself, because economic, political and social factors

also influence advancement. Education is necessary but not sufficient to group uplift. We will not put in place a world-class cultural infrastructure for our group unless we are very well educated and engaged in higher order critical thinking and problem solving. We will not put in place a world-class cultural infrastructure unless we know where we fit in the sweep of human history and more explicitly, how we want to shape our future, and what it will take to do it."

The vast majority of our children in rural and urban America attend public schools. It was, in fact, our Ancestors who, during the Reconstruction period, fought for and put into place legislation mandating free compulsory public education for all children. We must work to ensure the quality and sustainability of public schools in this nation, and repel all efforts to undermine and underfund them.

Chartered public schools offer new and compelling means of securing control of the education of our children. Designed by educators, parents and community partners, charter schools are autonomous, publicly-funded learning environments that are specifically tailored to meet the needs of particular students.[6]

Schools can be robust hubs of community life in the many hours of the day and night when students are not in their classes- offering workforce and career aptitude and readiness programs, computer labs, gymnasiums and playing fields, counseling and testing, and one-stop social service delivery. These services will bring adults into the schools, and help to foster the parental and community engagement in education that helps so much in attaining high student achievement.

In the attempt to meet the mandate of government to provide an excellent education to each of its children, public policy was established in the 1990's creating public schools that are independent, accepting higher accountability standards in exchange for autonomy. The policy environments for chartered public schools differ from state to state, so it is necessary to study exactly what the law dictates in each community.[7] African-centered charter schools can be exemplars of the ways in which this change in public policy can be utilized to manage and control the educations of our children. However, our blueprint must also include village-based after school learning environments where our culture, history and blueprint for living are taught, as well as where study groups for academic study—preschool through graduate and professional school—are conducted.   Lifelong learning, literacy, proficiency in mathematics, science and technology, and career readiness, in addition to cultural studies, should be the focus of our village-based after school learning centers.

Herma was most interested in the next institution: Governance is control of the laws, regulations and resources of the society. In the U.S., there are, at least theoretically, checks and balances among the three branches of government (executive, legislative, and courts). The Executive Branch is comprised of the President and everyone he appoints or hires. The Senate and House of Representatives (the Congress) make up the federal legislature—those who make the laws. And the Supreme Court has the final judicial word. At the state level, the Governor, State Legislature and state courts fulfill these three functions. At the municipal level, the Mayor, City Council (there are other names for this role) and local courts are responsible for governance.[8]

What happens at the neighborhood level?
We should be asking our community, what happens at the neighborhood level? Who is monitoring those who govern our city, county and state to be sure the interests of our group are met? We must ask ourselves: When we have an agreedupon agenda for governance, how will it become a part of the larger societal structure?

Our blueprint must reflect very careful thinking about governance. Who will provide leadership of our cultural renewal processes themselves, how will we guide ourselves through the consensus-building processes that will be required, and who will coordinate the work of implementation and ongoing cultural examination?

As a group within a larger group, we will need groupspecific leaders and thinkers who will take our combined views and form that group thought into a specific vision with goals and objectives that we can agree to and share. We need these leaders at the neighborhood, city, county, state, federal and international levels. In the spirit of democracy, which is our particular strength, we should elect these leaders and thinkers, and then walk with them every step of the way along the path to the fulfillment of our goals.

Tom became more intense: "In addition to leading and guiding our own group development, there must be leadership to connect us appropriately to the larger society. The in-group leader may not have the same qualities we will need in a societal leader—but our societal leader must represent our group decisions and protect our group interests in accordance with our agreed-upon agenda, vision and goals. We must recruit, train, groom, and financially sponsor the candidates who will represent us in this way." Those whom we elect must be accountable to the group. Therefore, it is also incumbent upon us to decide, before the fact, how we reward and how we punish the behavior of our political leaders and those who govern. Accountability is not something we can make up as we go along, yet situations will always arise which we have not considered or confronted before. The more clear and specific our agreements with one another are about our agenda, vision and goals, the better our chances of successfully enforcing accountability. General statements like "Do your best to represent the interests of the group" will not be very helpful— anyone can interpret that pretty much any way he or she wants to. On the other hand, a statement such as "Never enter into an agreement that has implications for the group without consulting with the in-group leadership team" is clear and unequivocal.

How do we feel about the difference between an elected leader's personal life and his or her public life? What are we prepared to do about an elected leader who puts his or her personal interests above those of the group? How do our rules and expectations relate to African-descended people who have not chosen to be part of our village? These and many other questions must be discussed, together, and decisions and consensus reached.

Let's talk about Faith
Everyone looked to Marguerite for the next institutional thoughts: "Faith and worship have been central to the identity of African-descended people since antiquity." The earliest writings we have found, from the Nile Valley civilizations at least three millennia ago, are highly developed spiritual treatises and clearly reveal that the thought that preceded the sacred scrolls had been developing over many decades, if not centuries, among the Nubian people. We introduced the concept of Maat earlier in our study group.

Perhaps it is useful to consider a distinction between spirituality and religion, for our purposes in studying how to renew our culture. Both spirituality and religion are about belief in the existence of a greater power than that of the human—the power that controls life on this planet and in this universe. Spirituality addresses the spirit or soul; religion is a particular system of faith and worship. To achieve the unity we must have as African-descended people, it will be important to understand that the truth of our spiritual belief and faith can transcend the differing religious systems to which many of us subscribe.

Most of the world's religions share a few tenets in common: there is one God; this Creator of each and every human being has vested in us a connection to the divine source, a spark of divinity; through faith in God, and because of our own oneness with the Creator, each of us can envision the life we want and actually bring it into being.

The law of cause and effect teaches us that what we reap, we sow. The seeds we plant are the seeds that grow in our lives. If we plant seeds of righteousness, fidelity and good will, we will enjoy these fruits. If we plant seeds of negativity, selfishness and treachery, we will suffer these scourges. Let us plant seeds of unity, consensus, confidence, order, intentionality and purpose, courage, determination, knowledge, expertise, success and victory! Let us plant the seeds of the Nguzo Saba and the Ethics of Sharing.[9] Let us plant seeds of the principles we agree to uphold together. We will achieve them.

For the purposes of our cultural revolution, let us focus on these spiritual tenets, rather than on particular religions. Let us focus on the great promise of faith, that we will decide upon a matter, and it shall be established for us![10] Let us depend on our ancient relationship to the Creator to guide us through the processes of cultural renewal and the uplift of our race. Let us look to the Creator and the Ancestors as we establish our cultural infrastructure and systems of accountability, individually, within our extended families and communities, and throughout our global village.

Economic Independence
Tom could hardly wait to speak about economic independence: Systems of commerce, wealth-building and employment are absolutely critical to our well-being. Economic exploitation has been the bane of our existence since the advent of the slave trade, and it still is—all around the planet.

We must put in place the means of providing for ourselves and putting much more of the $750 million in capital that flows through our hands like water each year to our own use. Estimates of the number of times one dollar is turned over within the white and Asian communities are four to six times greater than in our community. Every dollar we get should turn over in our own community at least four times.

There are at least three components to this imperative: supporting our own businesses; punishing our enemies through boycotts and selective buying campaigns; and business development—starting new enterprises that meet the needs of our group (and/or all people) where they do not already exist. Job creation, job-readiness, training and skills-banking are key aspects of the initiative as well.

Think about how you spend your money. Are your vendors for banking, education, merchandise, professional help, and services African-descended people? To the extent that you can, spend your money with your own people. Take note of the areas where you cannot spend with your own because goods or services are not available, or are not of the quality you require. We will want to plan means of filling these gaps and insisting upon higher performance.

Think about how you spend your money. Are there companies that offend us and our agenda, whose products you still buy? Are there companies that undermine our agenda by violating labor or environmental standards, by experimenting on "third world" women and children, or by "dumping" toxic, unsafe or useless products into the markets of our people around the world? Don't spend your money with such corporations. When an actual boycott is called because of an egregious breach, honor the boycott. Engage consciously and conscientiously in selective buying.

In addition to the need for work and a living wage for everyone who wants to work in our community, asset development is another critical area for our focus and collective action. Building wealth begins with saving some percentage of every dollar we receive. No wealth building plan can succeed unless there is a solid foundation of saving. For most, the greatest asset is homeownership. Truly, homeownership is the cornerstone of future wealth. African American homeownership in the U.S. has been stuck at 47 percent for several years, while white homeownership is above 73 percent Good credit is the single most important factor in qualifying for buying a home. The current housing crisis and economic downturn, and rising unemployment that hits our community especially hard, must be the focus of group-conscious interventions. What are we going to do about it?

Our blueprint must include saving and financial literacy, credit and homebuyer counseling, selective buying, investment clubs, cooperative ownership of homes and businesses, international trade, and entrepreneurship and business ownership brought to large scale.

A Blueprint for Law and Justice
Buddy had been waiting for someone to address his biggest concern, and Ra did: "Law and justice are often the subjects of greatest concern to African American young adults, and rightly so, because of the unconscionable numbers of young people who are under the control of the criminal justice system."[11]   Laws that require judges to impose mandatory minimum sentences for the sale of crack cocaine, but not for powder cocaine, discriminate in their effects against people of color. Crack is the drug of the streets and powder is the drug of the suites. The single cause of the dreadful increase in the numbers of young men and women who are incarcerated for nonviolent first offenses is the so-called "war on drugs" and in particular these mandatory minimum sentences. It is also true that young African Americans are harassed, interrogated, brutalized, arrested, convicted, and given longer sentences than their white counterparts, for the same crimes.[12]

Older African American adults often cite crime among the issues of greatest importance to them. Violent crime in our communities is most often perpetrated by us against us. Networks of warring gangs can destabilize neighborhoods and terrorize younger and older residents mercilessly.

Our blueprint in the area of law and justice must be at least three-pronged: the safety and security of everyone in our homes and neighborhoods through agreed upon neighborhood watch and community policing programs; aggressive support interventions for young people, including excellent schools, after school programs, mentoring and work experiences, and community-based alternatives to incarceration beginning with pre-sentencing representation; and a vigorous public information campaign to address egregious discrimination in criminal justice policy and practice, including moratoriums on the death penalty at the state and federal levels.

Buddy wanted to help plan what MI would do in terms of the criminal justice system (which he called the criminal punishment system). He told Ra he wanted to work with him on that.

Health and well-being
Then Marguerite continued: "Health, so central to our ability to function and pursue our goals, is often taken for granted." We have been endowed by the Creator with a body whose every cell is alive with divine intelligence and purpose, and whose life-sustaining operations like breathing are autonomic. When we take care of our bodies, and do not abuse, neglect or violate them, good health is the predictable outcome.[13] Diet, rest, exercise, and maintaining a harmonious, stress-free environment are fundamental aspects of taking care of ourselves.

We have lived under great stress for centuries! In the 21st century, it is very important to keep up with new health-related research findings and not simply do what our forbearers did with respect to these fundamentals, particularly in the fields of nutrition and stress management.

In our community, we can get out and work together to prevent disease and the transmission and spread of disease. Our robust and positive cultural revolution will itself help to bring harmony and reduce stress in our environment. We must ensure that our communities have culturally competent, highly skilled health care providers and that our families have access to quality, affordable health care services. We should get behind the public policy initiatives that are designed to reduce disparities in the health conditions of our people. We should become strong advocates in favor of healthy lifestyles and against destructive habits and practices, within our families and communities. Particular focus should be given to a cultural and age-appropriate set of messages directed to our young people, about good nutrition, the importance of exercise, childhood obesity, substance abuse, sexual activity, protection from sexually-transmitted diseases, decisions about family formation, and domestic violence.

No 21st century blueprint for group advancement would be complete without a well-developed infrastructure for healthy living—health of mind, body, and spirit.

Sol noted that recreation, arts and entertainment, self- and group-defense, non profit organizations (non-governmental organizations or civil society), and the media are other key components for discussion and organization.

Our 21st Century Village will have many dimensions
Ra concluded the session: "Our 21st Century Village will have many dimensions." It will exist in the mind of one or of many. It will be experienced electronically as well as personally and in groups. Its reality will be multi-media in every sense of the word. But what if we decide to also make take it live in particular times and places? What would it look like? This will be the topic of our next study group session, so give some real thought to what you would like to see in our Village.

Aida invited everyone to stay, listen to some music, have some good food and relax after this pretty grueling session. It was good to just enjoy each other's company, laugh, dance a little, laugh some more. The MI team went home in the wee hours of the morning, feeling like they had accomplished something good.

Buddy was struck by the question, "What is it that you do want? We know what you don't want; but what do you want?" He spent the week between sessions thinking about that challenge every chance he got.

Ra wasted no time when the session finally started: "What if we wanted to establish an African-centered cultural village in our community?" That could be the way to Achieve Our Collective Greatness Now. Where would we start? It would be helpful to begin by completing or updating an "asset map"[14] of the institutions and services that already exist in the community; and to assess the effectiveness of the existing assets, including a "gap analysis" of what does not exist or perform effectively. What would your checklist of priorities comprise? What's missing?

Envision the Village within your community, as you would ideally want it to be. Marguerite was first to give voice to her thoughts: "Symbols, representations, written and spoken statements and affirmations define the agreed-upon cultural values, accountability structures, and aesthetic of the Village." They can be seen, felt, heard, tasted, smelled, and spiritually sensed, unmistakably and unequivocally, throughout the Village. We must see art, hear music, experience rituals and uphold our values through text, images, art, music, our clothing, home decor, and institutional appointments.

Buddy did not wait to let everyone know what he had been thinking: "Every child without a functional family has a place in the residential heart of the Village, as do teachers, social workers, community builders, community police, entrepreneurs and other adults for whom affordable housing would be a blessing." The Village provides enrichment activities, structured interventions, and alternatives to incarceration for those with special needs, and for first-time juvenile and young adult offenders, including residential placements as needed.

Herma strongly agreed with Buddy and added: "There are support services for every family, including career readiness, conflict resolution, financial management, home economics, and a one-stop-shop facility for all government services." In addition to a health clinic, there are affordable preventive health practices, nutrition, and other services continually building a culture of wellness throughout the Village.

Sol was excited: "Education is central to the organization of the village." A school or schools serve children from early childhood through high school graduation, and serve adults in a robust program of lifelong learning and preparation for careers. In school, before and after school, African-centered studies, hands-on team learning, study groups, and other modes of group-conscious intellectual development occur. Everyone in the Village is, or will become, literate in at least one language, mathematics, and technology—100 percent.

Ra rejoined the discussion: "When we establish an actual prototype of the Village, others will want to build one too." In some communities, artistic and/or athletic programs will be emphasized. In others, the focus may be on agriculture, the environment and natural, organic, or green product production. Some communities may want their Villages to specialize in leadership development, systems change, the global economy, or communications. We will start a process of cultural renewal that will spread to other communities as well—maybe even globally!

Tom was enthusiastic: "The leaders communities elect in their Villages will reflect their priorities, their vision and mission, and what needs to be done." It's their job to protect the people and the resources of the Village. Remember that the in-group leaders and the leaders who will be needed to represent the Village and community in the larger societal contexts probably will not be the same. How will the group of leaders who negotiate the differences between the ingroup leaders and the representatives in the larger world, be chosen—and what will their responsibilities consist of? What was the ancient Council of Elders, and what were its purposes—and would their roles and functions be strictly internal to the Village in the 21st century? Can there be younger voices at this table in the contemporary Village? What is the difference between consensus and "majority rule"? Good governance, democratic governance, will be the *sine qua non* of the success of the Village. There was much discussion about Tom's excellent points, well into the night. The MI team decided they would transform their community into the 21st Century Village. If not they, who? If not now, when? We have a great Vision to share!

That very night, they decided upon a plan of action and divided the duties among them. First, each team member would begin talks with family members and their own circles of friends and associates, to build a level of awareness of the need for the effort. They would prepare a manual spelling out the cultural offensive and its logical conclusion: establishing the village.

They would ask for time on the agendas of meetings of groups they belonged to. They would ask for the support of all of their own groups; then they would go together to larger community meetings, faith centers, and neighborhood associations. Civic associations and the ecumenical faith leaders pledged their support. Educators and social service providers eagerly joined the campaign. Aida had friends in the political arena, and in media. When they were ready, the MI team members made presentations to all of them. The neighborhood papers carried their op ed articles, and after a while a supportive editorial appeared. Their strongest media support came from the radio stations most people in the community listened to—the on-air personalities made the cultural offensive and building the village for the community their own mission as well; meetings and events were covered, and fundraising was launched. Entrepreneurs and business people, architects and planners, developers and bankers began to draw up the blueprint and the plan for its implementation. They took the cause to local politicians and policy-makers and insisted upon their commitment to make it happen.

A Vision Realized
A year after the night of decision, becoming a culturally-defined 21st century village was a vision and intention shared by a critical mass of the community, and professional planning and fund-raising were underway. The planning process was run democratically; and was based upon the guiding principles and values of the cultural offensive. Everyone who participated affirmed their agreement to the rules, and to be held accountable for their compliance.

Over the next three years, even as the resources for the completed village were being identified and secured, the MI team completed key infrastructural objectives:

- the asset map of every resource for children in the community was drawn and put up on the website;

- every child from their community who was in protective services, who was homeless, or who needed additional support in foster care, was matched with at least one caring adult and mentor;

- negotiations with the Chief Judge of juvenile court had resulted in a phased-in intervention beginning with pre-sentencing, that would lead to a permanent alternative to incarceration for their first-time juvenile offenders, led by community- and faith-based organizations;

- educators, teachers, parents, and social service providers applied for and were granted a charter to begin the W.E.B. Du Bois Academy Public Charter School. School for grades pre-school through three would begin the next fall; and the school would add a grade each year, only admitting children into the earlier grades each year until the first of the original classes reached 12th grade;

- a small residential program for young mothers and their infants and toddlers was made possible through city services, run by the leadership of the school;

- a robust, coordinated, program of after-school activities, sports, clubs, and competitive teams was put in place for children and young adults of all ages, based in recreation centers and in the community's public and private schools, at the college, and in faith centers;

- lodges, fraternities and sororities, social clubs, professional societies and caucuses, and generous, ordinary families and individual residents staffed the programs;

- the MI team spearheaded a drive to provide study groups in every subject area for students in middle school, high school, undergraduate college courses, and for those working on advanced degrees.

The community experienced a tremendous uplift, and outcomes for the young people were measureable and dramatic. They began to see that the mission was indeed inevitable, through their commitment, efforts, and faith!

Faced with the solidarity and demonstrated commitment of the community, politicians and leaders of the financial institutions got busy figuring out what combinations of public and private investments would be needed to complete the village. They calculated that 1,200 children needed permanent homes in the village, along with the caregivers, teachers and coaches, service providers, security, and maintenance personnel that would be needed.

The children could be housed in groups of eight with four adults caring for them — a married couple who were educators (in the broad sense of the term), a housekeeper, and a college student. Of course, everyone who came in direct contact with the children would undergo the most stringent level of background checks and clearances. Housing for the adults would be a mix of apartment buildings, single- and multiple-family homes, retail shops, business offices. The main house included the administrative offices, cafeteria and restaurant, game room, auditorium, an art gallery, and the library and computer center.

It was decided that a combination of unused land, affordable housing already administered by the city, and new state and federal resources would be earmarked to build the residential campus. Philanthropists and bankers structured gifts and loans such that the developers could build the housing, main house, health clinic, shops and recreation center. Members of the community were hired in large numbers for this work. The city placed all of its local, state, and federal services in one building on the campus a "one-stop" service center. One major donor, a former professional athlete who had grown up in the community, contributed the athletic fields, golf course, tennis courts, and gymnasium, and an endowment to guarantee the resources for personnel and equipment, maintenance, and upgrading would also be in place. The extension service of the land grant college provided the vegetable and flower gardens, and did the landscaping. Members of the community of professional musicians built and staffed a recording studio. A major restaurant chain partnered with community caterers and food service providers to establish and cafeteria and restaurant. The arts community rallied mightily and brought talent searches, exhibits, regularly scheduled performances, classes, plays, and concerts by well-known musicians and dancers to the campus. The village in this community became the venue of choice for the city's image makers and policy-shapers. They were seen in the restaurant for breakfast, lunch or dinner every day, at sporting events, in the gallery with the artists, at performances, and in the gardens with the children. There was a perpetual media watch. Other communities in the city and in other cities liked what they saw; and replication was underway. National media personalities, Members of Congress, members of the President's Cabinet, Governors, Fortune 100 corporate leaders, and dignitaries from other countries, visited the village and carried the message back to their jurisdictions. The First Family was invited to the ribbon-cutting.

It is now eight years later. The Mission Inevitable team, with the help of Aida and her networks of committed change agents, did in fact establish their Village. It is a comprehensive, safe, nurturing place where no child asks the terrible, heartrending Question: "What difference does it make whether I live or die?"

Our story started with the vision of that Village, and it ends there.
First on a small scale, then growing and expanding as we learn, we can establish 21st century villages for our children and ourselves. Think about it. Talk about it. Envision it. Plan it. Organize. Believe. Work! Keep the Faith of the Ancestors. When will you begin?

If not we, then who! If not now, while we have an African American President of the United States, then when? If we are ready and willing, we are more than able to realize the perfect and unlimited equality of our group with any and all of the world's great races.

We can Achieve Our Collective Greatness Now!

APPENDIX 1
BLACK GOLD BOOK LIST
RHETT LEWIS

Achebe	Chinua	1988	*A Man of the People*
Achebe	Chinua	1989	*Arrow of God*
Achebe	Chinua	1990	*Hopes and Impediments: Selected Essays*
Achebe	Chinua	1991	*Girls at War*
Achebe	Chinua	1994	*Things Fall Apart: A Novel*
Achebe	Chinua	1997	*Anthills of the Savannah*
Achebe	Chinua	2000	*The Trouble with Nigeria*
Achebe	Chinua	2001	*Home and Exile*
Achebe	Chinua	2004	*Collected Poems*
Achebe	Chinua & C. L. Innes	1988	*African Short Stories*
Achebe	Chinua & J. Milne	2005	*No Longer at Ease: Intermediate*
Angelou	Maya	1978	*And Still I Rise*
Angelou	Maya	1991	*All God's Children Need Traveling Shoes*
Angelou	Maya	1993	*Life Doesn't Frighten Me*
Angelou	Maya	1994	*The Complete Collected Poems of Maya Angelou*
Angelou	Maya	1994	*Wouldn't Take Nothing for My Journey Now*
Angelou	Maya	1995	*Phenomenal Woman: Four Poems Celebrating Women*
Angelou	Maya	1996	*Maya Angelou: Poems*
Angelou	Maya	1998	*Even the Stars Look Lonesome*
Angelou	Maya	2003	*A Song Flung Up to Heaven*
Angelou	Maya	2003	*My Painted House, My Friendly Chicken, and Me*
Angelou	Maya	2004	*The Collected Autobiographies of Maya Angelou*
Angelou	Maya	2004	*Hallelujah! The Welcome Table: A Lifetime of Memories with Recipes*
Angelou	Maya	2006	*Celebrations: Rituals of Peace and Prayer*
Angelou	Maya	2006	*Mother: A Cradle to Hold Me*
Angelou	Maya	2008	*Letter to My Daughter*
Angelou	Maya	2008	*Amazing Peace: A Christmas Poem*
Angelou	Maya	2009	*I Know Why the Caged Bird Sings*
Angelou	Maya	2009	*The Heart of a Woman*
Angelou	Maya	2009	*Gather Together in My Name*
Armah	Ayi Kwei	1974	*Why Are We So Blest*

Armah	Ayi Kwei	1988	*The Beautyful Ones Are Not Yet Born*
Armah	Ayi Kwei	1995	*Fragments*
Armah	Ayi Kwei	1995	*Osiris rising: A novel of Africa past, present, and future*
Armah	Ayi Kwei	2000	*Two Thousand Seasons*
Armah	Ayi Kwei	2000	*The Healers*
Armah	Ayi Kwei	2002	*Kmt: In The House Of Life*
Armah	Ayi Kwei	2006	*The Eloquence of the Scribes: A Memoir on the Sources and Resources of African Literature*
Asante	Molefi Kete	1980	*A guide to African and African-American art*
Asante	Molefi Kete	1994	*Classical Africa*
Asante	Molefi Kete	1996	*African Intellectual Heritage*
Asante	Molefi Kete	1998	*Afrocentric Idea Revised*
Asante	Molefi Kete	1999	*African American History*
Asante	Molefi Kete	2000	*The Egyptian Philosophers: Ancient African Voices from Imhotep to Akhenaten*
Asante	Molefi Kete	2003	*Afrocentricity: The theory of Social Change*
Asante	Molefi Kete	2003	*Erasing Racism: The Survival of the American Nation*
Asante	Molefi Kete	2003	*100 Greatest African Americans: A Biographical Encyclopedia*
Asante	Molefi Kete	2005	*Race, Rhetoric, And Identity: The Architecton Of Soul*
Asante	Molefi Kete	2007	*An Afrocentric Manifesto*
Asante	Molefi Kete	2007	*The History of Africa: The Quest for Eternal Harmony*
Asante	Molefi Kete	2007	*Cheikh Anta Diop: An Intellectual Portrait*
Asante	Molefi Kete & Ama Mazama	2002	*Egypt vs. Greece and the American Academy*
Asante	Molefi Kete & Ama Mazama	2004	*Encyclopedia of Black Studies*
Asante	Molefi Kete & Ama Mazama	2008	*Encyclopedia of African Religion*
Asante	Molefi Kete & Dhyana Ziegler	1992	*Thunder and Silence: The Mass Media in Africa*

Asante	Molefi Kete & Kariamu Asante-Welsh	1989	African Culture the Rhythms of Unity
Asante	Molefi Kete, Augusta Mann, and Michael Webb	2001	Activity Book for African American History : A Journey of Liberation
Baldwin	James	1984	Notes of a Native Son
Baldwin	James	1985	The Price of the Ticket
Baldwin	James	1992	Another Country
Baldwin	James	1992	Nobody Knows My Name
Baldwin	James	1994	Sonny's Blues
Baldwin	James	1995	Going to Meet the Man: Stories
Baldwin	James	1995	The Evidence of Things Not Seen
Baldwin	James	1995	Blues for Mister Charlie: A Play
Baldwin	James	1998	James Baldwin : Collected Essays : Notes of a Native Son / Nobody Knows My Name / The Fire Next Time / No Name in the Street / The Devil Finds Work / Other Essays
Baldwin	James	1998	Tell Me How Long the Train's Been Gone
Baldwin	James	1998	The Amen Corner: A Play
Baldwin	James	2000	Go Tell It on the Mountain
Baldwin	James	2000	Giovanni's Room
Baldwin	James	2000	Just Above My Head
Baldwin	James	2000	The Fire Next Time
Baldwin	James	2000	The Devil Finds Work: Essays
Baldwin	James	2004	Vintage Baldwin
Baldwin	James	2006	If Beale Street Could Talk
Baldwin	James	2007	No Name in the Street
Baldwin	James	2007	One Day When I Was Lost
Baldwin	James	2009	Fifty Famous Stories Retold
Barnes	Carol	2001	Melanin: The Chemical Key To Black Greatness
Bell	Derrick	1989	And We Are Not Saved: The Elusive Quest For Racial Justice
Bell	Derrick	1993	Faces At The Bottom Of The Well: The Permanence Of Racism
Bell	Derrick	1997	Gospel Choirs: Psalms Of Survival In An Alien Land Called Home
Bell	Derrick	2003	Ethical Ambition : Living a Life of Meaning and Worth
Bell	Derrick	2005	Silent Covenants: Brown v. Board of Education and the Unfulfilled Hopes for Racial Reform
Bell	Derrick	2008	Race, Racism & American Law

Ben-Jochannan	Yosef A. A.	Black Man of the Nile
Ben-Jochannan	Yosef A. A.	The Myth of Exodus and Genesis and the Exclusion of Their African Origins
Ben-Jochannan	Yosef A. A.	A Chronology of the Bible: Challenge to the Standard Version
Ben-Jochannan	Yosef A. A.	African Origins of Major "Western Religions"
Ben-Jochannan	Yosef A. A.	Cultural Genocide in the Black and African Studies Curriculum
Ben-Jochannan	Yosef A. A.	We, the Black Jews: Witness to the 'White Jewish Race' Myth, Volumes I & II (in One)
Ben-Jochannan	Yosef A. A.	Africa: Mother of Western Civilization
Ben-Jochannan	Yosef A. A.	The Black Man's North and East Africa
Ben-Jochannan	Yosef A. A.	The Need for a Black Bible
Ben-Jochannan	Yosef A. A.	Our Black Seminarians and Black Clergy Without a Black Theology
Ben-Jochannan	Yosef A. A.	Axioms and quotations of Yosef Ben-Jochannan
Ben-Jochannan	Yosef A. A.	The African Mysteries System of wa'set, Egypt and Its European Stepchild: "Greek Philosophy"
Ben-Jochannan	Yosef A. A.	The African Called Rameses and the Origin of Western Civilization
Ben-Jochannan	Yosef A. A.	Understanding the African Philosophical Concept Behind the "Diagram of the Law of Opposites"
Ben-Jochannan	Yosef A. A.	Doc Ben speaks out (Monograph series / Alkebu-lan Historical Research Society)
Ben-Jochannan	Yosef A. A.	Abu Simbel to Ghizeh: A Guide Book and Manual
Ben-Jochannan	Yosef A. A.	"They all look alike! all of them"?: From Egypt to Papua New Guinea
Ben-Jochannan	Yosef A. A.	In pursuit of George G.M. James' study of African origins in "Western Civilization"
Ben-Jochannan	Yosef A. A.	The Alkebu-lanians of Ta-Merry's "mysteries system," and the ritualization of the late Bro. Kwesie Adebisi

Ben-Jochannan	Yosef A. A.		*From Afrikan Captives to Insane Slaves: The Need for Afrikan History in Solving the "Black" Mental Health Crisis in "America" and the World (Truth & Sanity Reprint Series)*
Ben-Jochannan	Yosef A. A.		*THE SAGA OF THE 'BLACK MARXISTS' VERSUS THE 'BLACK NATIONALISTS': A DEBATE RESURRECTED VOLUME/BOOK I, II, III*
Ben-Jochannan	Yosef A. A.		*Influence of great myths of contemporary life: Or, The need for Black history im mental health : a sociopolitical and anthropological student's and researcher's ... (Black mental illness and the Bicentennial)*
Ben-Jochannan	Yosef A. A.		*Tutankhamun's African roots Haley, et al, overlooked! ?*
Ben-Jochannan	Yosef A. A.		*A brief chronology of the development and history of the Old and New Testament: From its African and Asian origins to its European and European-American ... etc (African-American heritage series)*
Ben-Jochannan	Yosef A. A.		*The Black man's religion, and Extracts and comments from the Holy Black Bible (African-American heritage series)*
Ben-Jochannan	Yosef A. A.		*Africa; lands, peoples, and cultures of the world*
Bennett	Lerone, Jr.	1965	*What Manner of Man, a Biography of Martin Lurter King, Jr*
Bennett	Lerone, Jr.	1968	*Pioneers in Protest*
Bennett	Lerone, Jr.	1968	*Confrontation: Black and White*
Bennett	Lerone, Jr.	1969	*Black Power U.S.A.*
Bennett	Lerone, Jr.	1972	*The Challenge of Blackness*
Bennett	Lerone, Jr.	1992	*Great Moments In Black History (Wade in the Water)*
Bennett	Lerone, Jr.		*Forced into Glory: Abraham Lincoln's White Dream*
Bennett	Lerone, Jr.		*Before the Mayflower: A History of Black America*

Bennett	Lerone, Jr. & Ebony	1971	*Ebony Pictorial History of Black America (3 Volume Set)*
Bennett	Lerone, Jr., Benny Andrews, Vincent Harding and Lucy R. Lippard Dr.Mary Schmidt Campbell	1985	*Tradition and Conflict: Images of a Turbulent Decade 1963-1973*
Berry	Mary Frances	1977	*Military Necessity and Civil Rights Policy: Black Citizenship and the Constitution, 1861-1868*
Berry	Mary Frances	1986	*Why Era Failed: Politics, Women's Rights, and the Amending Process of the Constitution*
Berry	Mary Frances	1994	*The Politics of Parenthood: Child Care, Women's Rights, and the Myth of the Good Mother*
Berry	Mary Frances	1995	*Black Resistance/White Law: A History of Constitutional Racism in America*
Berry	Mary Frances	2000	*The Pig Farmer's Daughter and Other Tales of American Justice: Episodes of Racism and Sexism in the Courts from 1865 to the Present*
Berry	Mary Frances	2006	*My Face Is Black Is True: Callie House and the Struggle for Ex-Slave Reparations*
Berry	Mary Frances	2009	*And Justice for All: The United States Commission on Civil Rights and the Continuing Struggle for Freedom in America*
Berry	Mary Frances & John W. Blassingame	1982	*Long Memory: The Black Experience in America*
Berry	Mary Frances, Cruz Reynoso, and Carl A. Anderson	2004	*Racial And Ethnic Tensions In American Communities: Poverty, Inequality, And Discrimination - A National Perspective*
Blake	Dorothy	2001	*Yakub & The Origins Of White Supremacy: Message To The White Man & Woman In America*
Blassingame	James W.		*The Slave Community: Plantation Life in the Antebellum South*
Bontemps	Arna Wendell	1955	*Story of the Negro*

Bontemps	Arna Wendell	1992	*Black Thunder: Gabriel's Revolt: Virginia, 1800*
Bontemps	Arna Wendell	2005	*God Sends Sunday: A Novel*
Bontemps	Arna Wendell, Charles Harold Nichols, and Langston Hughes	1990	*Arna Bontemps-Langston Hughes Letters, 1925-1967*
Brooks	Gwendolyn	1963	*Selected Poems; Gwendolyn Brooks*
Brooks	Gwendolyn	1989	*Annie Allen*
Brooks	Gwendolyn	1991	*Primer for Blacks*
Brooks	Gwendolyn	1992	*Maud Martha: A Novel*
Brooks	Gwendolyn	1994	*Blacks*
Brooks	Gwendolyn	2003	*In Montgomery: And Other Poems*
Brooks	Gwendolyn	2006	*Selected Poems*
Brooks	Gwendolyn	2006	*Bronzeville Boys and Girls*
Brooks	Gwendolyn	2008	*People of the Book: A Novel*
Browder	Anthony T.	1992	*Nile Valley Contributions to Civilization*
Browder	Anthony T.	1994	*Nile Valley Contributions to Civilization Workbook*
Browder	Anthony T.	1995	*Africa on My Mind*
Browder	Anthony T.	1996	*From the Browder File: Survival Strategies for Africans in America 13 Steps to Freedom*
Browder	Anthony T.	2004	*Egypt on the Potomac*
Butler	Kim	1998	*Freedoms Given, Freedoms Won: Afro-Brazilians in Post-Abolition Sao Paulo and Salvador*
Butler	Octavia E.	1979	*Survivor*
Butler	Octavia E.	1979	*Patternmaster*
Butler	Octavia E.	1988	*Dawn*
Butler	Octavia E.	1994	*Mind of My Mind*
Butler	Octavia E.	1996	*Clay's Ark*
Butler	Octavia E.	1997	*Parable of the Talents*
Butler	Octavia E.	1997	*Imago*
Butler	Octavia E.	2000	*Lilith's Brood*
Butler	Octavia E.	2000	*Parable of the Sower*
Butler	Octavia E.	2001	*Wild Seed*
Butler	Octavia E.	2003	*Parable of the Talents*
Butler	Octavia E.	2004	*Kindred*

Butler	Octavia E.	2007	*Fledgling*
Butler	Octavia E.	2007	*Seed to Harvest*
Butler	Octavia E.		*Adulthood Rites: Xenogenesis*
Cabral	Amilcar	1969	*The struggle in Guinea*
Cabral	Amilcar	1970	*Revolution in Guinea: Selected Texts*
Cabral	Amilcar	1974	*Return to the Source: Selected Speeches*
Cabral	Amilcar	1979	*Unity and Struggle: Speeches and Writings*
Chinweizu		1975	*The West and the Rest of Us: White Predators, Black Slavers and the African Elite*
Chinweizu		1986	*Invocations and admonitions: 49 poems and a triptych of parables*
Chinweizu		1987	*Decolonising the African mind*
Chinweizu		1989	*Voices from Twentieth Century Africa: Griots and Town Criers*
Chinweizu		1990	*Anatomy of female power: A masculinist dissection of matriarchy*
Chinweizu		1998	*Toward the Decolonization of African Literature*
Clarke	John Henrik		*Christopher Columbus and the Afrikan Holocaust: Slavery and the Rise of European Capitalism*
Clarke	John Henrik		*Who Betrayed the African World Revolution?: And Other Speeches*
Clarke	John Henrik		*Africans at the Crossroads: African World Revolution*
Clarke	John Henrik		*Marcus Garvey and the Vision of Africa*
Clarke	John Henrik		*Black American Short Stories*
Clarke	John Henrik		*My Life in Search of Africa*
Clarke	John Henrik		*Malcolm X: The Man and His Times*
Clarke	John Henrik		*African People in World History*
Clarke	John Henrik		*New Dimensions in African History*
Clarke	John Henrik		*Christopher Columbus and the African Holocaust: Slavery and the Rise of European Capitalism*

Clarke	John Henrik	*Rebellion in Rhyme the Early Poetry of John Henrik Clarke*
Clarke	John Henrik	*HARLEM: A Community in Transition*
Clarke	John Henrik	*Freedomways: A Quarterly Review of the Negro Freedom Movement*
Clarke	John Henrik	*William Styron's Nat Turner. Ten Black Writers Respond*
Clarke	John Henrik	*Dimensions of the Struggle Against Apartheid. A Tribute to Paul Robeson. Held Under the Auspices of the United Nations Special Committee Against Apartheid, 10 April 1978*
Clarke	John Henrik	*Black Titan: W. E. B. Du Bois*
Clarke	John Henrik	*Social studies African-American baseline essay*
Clarke	John Henrik	*Harlem Voices from the Soul of Black America*
Clarke	John Henrik	*The influence of African cultural continuity on the slave revolts in South America and in the Caribbean islands*
Clarke	John Henrik	*Africans away from home*
Clarke	John Henrik	*Houses of Roman Italy, 100 BC AD 250; Ritual, Space, and Decoration*
Clarke	John Henrik	*Critical Lessons in Slavery and the Slave Trade : Essential Studies & Commentaries on Slavery, in General, & the African Slave Trade in Particular*
Clarke	John Henrik	*The nineteenth century roots of the African and Afro-American freedom struggle*
Clarke	John Henrik	*Ahmed Baba, a scholar of old Africa (The 1983 Afro-American history kit)*
Clarke	John Henrik	*The middle passage: Our holocaust! (A series of booklets)*

Clarke	John Henrik		Black/white alliances: A historical perspective
Clarke	John Henrik		The image of Africa in the mind of the Afro-American: African identity in the literature of struggle (Phelps-Stokes seminars on African-American relations)
Clarke	John Henrik		The Second Crucifixion of Nat Turner
Clarke	John Henrik & Alfred J. Butler		The Arab Invasion of Egypt: And the Last 30 Years of the Roman Dominion
Clarke	John Henrik & Tom Feelings		The Middle Passage: White Ships/ Black Cargo
Clarke	John Henrik & Vincent Harding		Black Heritage: Slave Trade and Slavery v. 2
Cole	Johnetta B.	1993	Conversations; straight talk with America's sister president
Cole	Johnetta B.	1997	Dream The Boldest Drems And Other Lessons Of Life
Cone	James H.	1984	For My People: Black Theology and the Black Church
Cone	James H.	1985	My Soul Looks Back
Cone	James H.	1990	A Black Theology of Liberation
Cone	James H.	1992	Martin & Malcolm & America: A Dream or a Nightmare
Cone	James H.	1992	The Spirituals and the Blues: An Interpretation
Cone	James H.	1997	God of the Oppressed
Cone	James H.	1997	Black Theology and Black Power
Cone	James H.	1999	Speaking the Truth: Ecumenism, Liberation, and Black Theology
Cone	James H.	2000	Risks of Faith: The Emergence of a Black Theology of Liberation, 1968-1998
Cone	James H. & Gayraud S. Wilmore	1993	Black Theology: A Documentary History : 1966-1979
Cone	James H. & Gayraud S. Wilmore	1993	Black Theology: A Documentary History [Volume Two: 1980-1992]
Cortez	Jayne	1969	Pissstained stairs and the monkey man's wares

Cortez	Jayne	1971	*Festivals and funerals*
Cortez	Jayne	1977	*Mouth on Paper*
Cortez	Jayne	1978	*Scarifications*
Cortez	Jayne	1982	*Firespitter*
Cortez	Jayne	1984	*Coagulations: New and Selected Poems*
Cortez	Jayne	1991	*Poetic Magnetic*
Cortez	Jayne	1996	*Somewhere In Advance of Nowhere*
Cortez	Jayne	2002	*Jazz Fan Looks Back*
Cortez	Jayne	2003	*Watts. Art And Social Change In Los Angeles 1965-2002*
Cortez	Jayne	2007	*The Beautiful Book*
Cortez	Jayne	2009	*On the Imperial Highway: New and Selected Poems*
Cruse	Harold	1968	*Crisis of the Negro Intellectual*
Cruse	Harold	1969	*Rebellion or Revolution Lucid and Eloquent Statements on the American Racial Impasse*
Cruse	Harold	1987	*Plural but Equal: A Critical Study of Blacks and Minorities and America's Plural*
Cushman,	Kathleen & Lisa D. Delpit	2005	*Fires in the Bathroom: Advice for Teachers from High School Students*
Danticat	Edwidge	1998	*Breath, Eyes, Memory*
Darling-Hammond	Linda	1990	*The Teaching Internship: Practical Preparation for a Licensed Profession*
Darling-Hammond	Linda	2000	*Solving the dilemmas of teacher supply, demand, and standards: How we can ensure a competent, caring, and qualified teacher for every child*
Darling-Hammond	Linda	2001	*The Right to Learn: A Blueprint for Creating Schools that Work*
Darling-Hammond	Linda	2006	*Powerful Teacher Education: Lessons from Exemplary Programs*

Darling-Hammond	Linda	2009	*The Flat World and Education: How America's Commitment to Equity Will Determine Our Future*
Darling-Hammond	Linda & Gary Sykes	2009	*Teaching as the Learning Profession: Handbook of Policy and Practice*
Darling-Hammond	Linda & Joan Baratz-Snowden	2005	*A Good Teacher in Every Classroom : Preparing the Highly Qualified Teachers Our Children Deserve*
Darling-Hammond	Linda & Judith Lanier	2005	*Professional Development Schools: Schools For Developing A Profession*
Darling-Hammond	Linda, Arthur E Wise, and Stephen P. Klein	1995	*A License To Teach: Building A Profession For 21st Century Schools*
Darling-Hammond	Linda, Arthur E Wise, and Stephen P. Klein	1999	*A License to Teach: Raising Standards for Teaching*
Darling-Hammond	Linda, Brigid Barron, P. David Pearson, and Alan H. Schoenfeld	2008	*Powerful Learning: What We Know About Teaching for Understanding*
Darling-Hammond	Linda, Debra Meyerson, Michelle LaPointe, and Margaret T. Orr	2009	*Preparing Principals for a Changing World: Lessons From Effective School Leadership Programs*
Darling-Hammond	Linda, Jacqueline Ancess, and Beverly Falk	1995	*Authentic Assessment in Action: Studies of Schools and Students at Work*
Darling-Hammond	Linda, Jennifer French, and Silvia Paloma Garcia-Lopez	2002	*Learning to Teach for Social Justice*
Darling-Hammond	Linda, John Bransford, Pamela LePage, and Karen Hammerness	2007	*Preparing Teachers for a Changing World: What Teachers Should Learn and Be Able to Do*
Delaney	Martin Robinson	1859	*Blake or The Huts of America*
Delaney	Martin Robinson	1859	*The Condition, Elevation, Emigration, and Destiny of the Colored People of the United States and Official Report of the Niger Valley Exploring Party*

Delaney	Martin Robinson	1879	*Principia of Ethnology*
Delaney	Martin Robinson		*The Origin of Races and Color*
Delaney	Martin Robinson		*The Beginnings of Black Nationalism*
Delpit	Lisa D.	2006	*Other People's Children: Cultural Conflict in the Classroom*
Delpit	Lisa D. & Joanne Kilgour Dowdy	2008	*The Skin That We Speak: Thoughts on Language and Culture in the Classroom*
Delpit	Lisa D., M. Christopher Brown, and Roderic R. Land	2005	*The Politics of Curricular Change: Race, Hegemony, and Power in Education*
Diop	Cheikh Anta	1976	*Technical co-operation among African countries: A survey of selected countries*
Diop	Cheikh Anta	1987	*Black Africa: The Economic and Cultural Basis for a Federated State*
Diop	Cheikh Anta	1988	*Precolonial Black Africa*
Diop	Cheikh Anta	1989	*The African Origin of Civilization: Myth or Reality*
Diop	Cheikh Anta	1990	*Cheikh Anta Diop: On science, history and technology*
Diop	Cheikh Anta	1991	*Civilization or Barbarism: An Authentic Anthropology*
Diop	Cheikh Anta	1997	*The Peopling of Ancient Egypt & the Deciphering of the Meroitic Script*
Diop	Cheikh Anta	2000	*The Cultural Unity of Black Africa: The Domains of Patriarchy and of Matriarchy in Classical Antiquity*
Diop	Cheikh Anta	2000	*Towards the African Renaissance: Essays in African Culture and Development, 1946-1960*
DuBois	W. E. B.	1954	*The Suppression of the African Slave-Trade to the United States of America 1638-1870*
DuBois	W. E. B.		*The Souls of Black Folk*
DuBois	W. E. B.		*The Education of Black People: Ten Critiques, 1906 - 1960*

DuBois	W. E. B.	*The Quest of the Silver Fleece: A Novel*
DuBois	W. E. B.	*Against Racism: Unpublished Essays, Papers, Addresses, 1887-1961*
DuBois	W. E. B.	*The Philadelphia Negro: A Social Study*
DuBois	W. E. B.	*Color and Democracy: Colonies and Peace*
DuBois	W. E. B.	*Black Folk Then and Now: An Essay Into the History and Sociology of the Black Race*
DuBois	W. E. B.	*Encyclopedia of the Negro: Preparatory Volume with Reference Lists and Reports*
DuBois	W. E. B.	*Amenia Conference: An Historic Negro Gathering*
DuBois	W. E. B.	*Darkwater Voices From Within the Veil*
DuBois	W. E. B.	*Dusk of Dawn: an Essay Toward an Autobiography of a Race Concept*
DuBois	W. E. B.	*The Negro American Family (The Atlantic University Publication Series)*
DuBois	W. E. B.	*Negro Social and Political Thought 1850-1920: Representative Texts*
DuBois	W. E. B.	*On this first day of October: Dr. W.E.B. DuBois' application to join the Communist Party and Gus Hall's reply*
DuBois	W. E. B.	*The Seventh Son (2 Volumes) The Thought and Writings of W. E. B. Du Bois*
DuBois	W. E. B.	*Three Essays - in Travels of The Black Atlantic (first book publication)*
DuBois	W. E. B.	*W. E. B. DuBois: the Crisis Writings*
DuBois	W. E. B.	*John Brown*
DuBois	W. E. B.	*Africa, Its Geography, People and Products*

DuBois	W. E. B.		*Dark Princess*
DuBois	W. E. B.		*Does Race Antipathy Serve Any Good Purpose?*
DuBois	W. E. B.		*W.E.B. Dubois Speaks: Speeches and Addresses 1920-1963*
DuBois	W. E. B. & David Levering Lewis		*Black Reconstruction in America, 1860-1880*
DuBois	W. E. B. & Herbert Aptheker		*Autobiography of W.E.B. DuBois, The: A Soliloquy on Viewing My Life from the Last Decade of Its First Century*
DuBois	W. E. B. & Robert Gregg		*The Negro*
Dunbar	Paul Laurence	1975	*The Paul Laurence Dunbar reader: A selection of the best of Paul Laurence Dunbar's poetry and prose, including writings never before available in book form*
Dunbar	Paul Laurence	1993	*The Collected Poetry of Paul Laurence Dunbar*
Dunbar	Paul Laurence	2002	*In His Own Voice: Dramatic & Other Uncollected Works*
Dunbar	Paul Laurence	2004	*Selected Poems*
Dunbar	Paul Laurence	2008	*The Complete Poems Of Paul Laurence Dunbar*
Dunbar	Paul Laurence	2009	*The Complete Stories of Paul Laurence Dunbar*
Dunbar	Paul Laurence	2009	*The Sport of the Gods*
Dyson	Michael Eric	1995	*Making Malcolm: The Myth and Meaning of Malcolm X*
Dyson	Michael Eric	2001	*I May Not Get There with You: The True Martin Luther King, Jr*
Dyson	Michael Eric	2002	*Open Mike: Reflections on Philosophy, Race, Sex, Culture and Religion*
Dyson	Michael Eric	2004	*Why I Love Black Women*
Dyson	Michael Eric	2005	*Mercy, Mercy Me: The Art, Loves and Demons of Marvin Gaye*

Dyson	Michael Eric	2006	*Is Bill Cosby Right?: Or Has the Black Middle Class Lost Its Mind?*
Dyson	Michael Eric	2006	*Holler If You Hear Me*
Dyson	Michael Eric	2007	*Debating Race: with Michael Eric Dyson*
Dyson	Michael Eric	2007	*Know What I Mean? : Reflections on Hip-Hop*
Dyson	Michael Eric	2007	*Come Hell or High Water: Hurricane Katrina and the Color of Disaster*
Dyson	Michael Eric	2008	*April 4, 1968: Martin Luther King Jr.'s Death and How It Changed America*
Dyson	Michael Eric	2009	*Can You Hear Me Now?: The Inspiration, Wisdom, and Insight of Michael Eric Dyson*
Dyson	Michael Eric	2009	*Full of the Hope That the Present Has Brought Us: Obama and America*
Feelings	Tom & Eloise Greenfield	1993	*Daydreamers*
Felder	Cain Hope	1989	*Troubling Biblical Waters: Race, Class, and Family*
Felder	Cain Hope	1990	*Lift Every Voice The Bible in an Age of diversity*
Felder	Cain Hope	1991	*Stony the Road We Trod: African American Biblical Interpretation*
Felder	Cain Hope	1992	*Proclamation: Interpreting the Lessons of the Church Year*
Felder	Cain Hope	1993	*Original African Heritage Study Bible*
Felder	Cain Hope	2002	*Race, Racism, and the Biblical Narratives*
Felder	Cain Hope	2007	*The Original African Heritage Study Bible: King James Version*
Felder	Cain Hope	2007	*True to Our Native Land: An African American New Testament Commentary*
Finch	Charles S.	1991	*Echoes of the Old Darkland: Themes from the African Eden*
Finch	Charles S.	1991	*Africa and the Birth of Science and Technology*

Finch	Charles S.	1998	*The Star of Deep Beginnings*
Finch	Charles S.	1999	*Biblio Africana: An Annotated Reader's Guide to African Cultural History and Related Subjects*
Finch	Charles S.	2000	*The African Background to Medical Science: Essays on African History, Science & Civilizations*
Franklin	John Hope & Alfred A. Moss Jr.		*From Slavery to Freedom: A History of African Americans (2 Vols. in 1)*
Frazier	Edward Franklin	1951	*Negro Family in the united States, Revised and Abridged Editon*
Frazier	Edward Franklin	1951	*The Negro in the United States*
Frazier	Edward Franklin	1957	*Black Bourgeoisie*
Frazier	Edward Franklin	1968	*The Free Negro Family : A Study of Family Origins Before the Civil War*
Frazier	Edward Franklin	1970	*The Negro Church in America*
Frazier	Edward Franklin, Eric Williams, Tony Martin, and Erica Williams Connell	2004	*The Economic Future of the Caribbean*
Freiere	Paulo	1970	*Pedagogy of the Oppressed*
Freiere	Paulo	1985	*The Politics of Education: Culture, Power and Liberation*
Freiere	Paulo	1987	*Literacy: Reading the Word and the World*
Freiere	Paulo	1996	*Letters to Cristina*
Freiere	Paulo	1998	*Pedagogy of the Heart*
Freiere	Paulo	2001	*Pedagogy of Freedom: Ethics, Democracy, and Civic Courage*
Freiere	Paulo	2004	*Pedagogy Of Hope: Reliving Pedagogy Of The Oppressed*
Freiere	Paulo	2005	*Education For Critical Consciousness*
Freiere	Paulo	2006	*Teachers As Cultural Workers: Letters to Those Who Dare Teach With New Commentary by Peter McLaren, Joe L. Kincheloe, and Shirley Steinberg Expanded Edition*
Freiere	Paulo, Donaldo Macedo, Ana Lucia Souza de Frietas, and Peter Park	2007	*Daring to Dream: Toward a Pedagogy of the Unfinished*
Freiere	Paulo, James W. Fraser, Donaldo Macedo, and Tanya McKinnon	1997	*Mentoring the Mentor: A Critical Dialogue With Paulo Freire*

Surname	Given	Year	Title
Garrow	David	2004	*Bearing the Cross: Martin Luther King, Jr., and the Southern Christian Leadership Conference*
Garvey	Amy Jacques	1977	*More Philosophy and Opinions of Marcus Garvey*
Garvey	Marcus	1984	*The Marcus Garvey and Universal Negro Improvement Association Papers, Vol. III: September 1920-August 1921*
Garvey	Marcus		*Message to the People: The Course of African Philosophy*
Garvey	Marcus		*Marcus Garvey Life and Lessons: A Centennial Companion to the Marcus Garvey and Universal Negro Improvement Association Papers*
Garvey	Marcus		*The Poetical Works of Marcus Garvey*
Garvey	Marcus & Amy Jacques Garvey		*The Philosophy and Opinions of Marcus Garvey, Or, Africa for the Africans*
Garvey	Marcus & Tony Martin	1986	*Message to the People: The Course of African Philosophy (New Marcus Garvey Library, Vol 7)*
Giovanni	Nikki	1974	*My House*
Giovanni	Nikki	1976	*Gemini: An Extended Autobiographical Statement My 1ST 20 5 Years Being Black Poet*
Giovanni	Nikki	1979	*The Women and the Men*
Giovanni	Nikki	1980	*Cotton Candy on a Rainy Day*
Giovanni	Nikki	1987	*Spin a Soft Black Song: Poems for Children*
Giovanni	Nikki	1988	*Black Feeling, Black Talk, Black Judgement*
Giovanni	Nikki	1993	*Ego-Tripping and Other Poems for Young People*
Giovanni	Nikki	1995	*Racism 101*
Giovanni	Nikki	1996	*The Sun Is So Quiet*
Giovanni	Nikki	1996	*The Selected Poems of Nikki Giovanni: 1968-1995*
Giovanni	Nikki	1996	*Grand Mothers: Poems, Reminiscences, and Short Stories About The Keepers Of Our Traditions*
Giovanni	Nikki	1997	*Love Poems*
Giovanni	Nikki	1998	*The Genie in the Jar*
Giovanni	Nikki	1999	*Grand Fathers: Reminiscences, Poems, Recipes, and Photos of the Keepers of Our Traditions*
Giovanni	Nikki	1999	*Blues: For All the Changes: New Poems*
Giovanni	Nikki	2002	*Quilting the Black-Eyed Pea: Poems and Not Quite Poems*
Giovanni	Nikki	2003	*The Prosaic Soul of Nikki Giovanni*
Giovanni	Nikki	2004	*Just For You! The Girls In The Circle*

Giovanni	Nikki	2007	*On My Journey Now: Looking at African-American History Through the Spirituals*
Giovanni	Nikki	2007	*Rosa*
Giovanni	Nikki	2007	*Acolytes: Poems*
Giovanni	Nikki	2007	*The Collected Poetry of Nikki Giovanni: 1968-1998*
Giovanni	Nikki	2008	*The Grasshopper's Song: An Aesop's Fable Revisited*
Giovanni	Nikki	2008	*Lincoln and Douglass: An American Friendship*
Giovanni	Nikki	2008	*Hip Hop Speaks to Children with CD: A Celebration of Poetry with a Beat*
Giovanni	Nikki	2009	*Bicycles: Love Poems*
Greenfield	Eloise	1991	*Lisa's Daddy and Daughter Day*
Greenfield	Eloise	1995	*Koya Delaney and the Good Girl Blues*
Greenfield	Eloise	1996	*Grandpa's Face*
Greenfield	Eloise	1997	*For The Love Of The Game: Michael Jordan And Me*
Greenfield	Eloise	1998	*Angels : An African-American Treasury*
Greenfield	Eloise	1999	*Grandmama's Joy*
Greenfield	Eloise & Amos Ferguson	1991	*Under the Sunday Tree*
Greenfield	Eloise & Carole Byard	1992	*Africa Dream*
Greenfield	Eloise & Floyd Cooper	1988	*Granpa's Face*
Greenfield	Eloise & George Cephas Ford	1980	*Darlene*
Greenfield	Eloise & George Ford	2009	*Paul Robeson*
Greenfield	Eloise & Gil Ashby	1995	*Rosa Parks*
Greenfield	Eloise & James Calvin	1991	*Talk About a Family*
Greenfield	Eloise & Jan Spivey Gilchrist	1991	*My Daddy and I*
Greenfield	Eloise & Jan Spivey Gilchrist	1991	*First Pink Light*
Greenfield	Eloise & Jan Spivey Gilchrist	1991	*Big Friend, Little Friend*
Greenfield	Eloise & Jan Spivey Gilchrist	1993	*Nathaniel Talking*
Greenfield	Eloise & Jan Spivey Gilchrist	1993	*William and the Good Old Days*
Greenfield	Eloise & Jan Spivey Gilchrist	1994	*Aaron and Gayla's Counting Book*
Greenfield	Eloise & Jan Spivey Gilchrist	1994	*Aaron and Gayla's Alphabet Book*
Greenfield	Spivey Gilchrist	1994	*Sweet Baby Coming*

	Author	Year	Title
Greenfield	Eloise & Jan Spivey Gilchrist	1995	*On My Horse*
Greenfield	Eloise & Jan Spivey Gilchrist	1996	*Night on Neighborhood Street*
Greenfield	Eloise & Jan Spivey Gilchrist	1997	*Kia Tanisha*
Greenfield	Eloise & Jan Spivey Gilchrist	1997	*Kia Tanisha Drives Her Car*
Greenfield	Eloise & Jan Spivey Gilchrist	1999	*Water, Water*
Greenfield	Eloise & Jan Spivey Gilchrist	2001	*I Can Draw a Weeposaur and Other Dinosaurs*
Greenfield	Eloise & Jan Spivey Gilchrist	2001	*Easter Parade*
Greenfield	Eloise & Jan Spivey Gilchrist	2002	*How They Got Over: African Americans and the Call of the Sea*
Greenfield	Eloise & Jan Spivey Gilchrist	2003	*In the Land of Words: New and Selected Poems*
Greenfield	Eloise & Jan Spivey Gilchrist	2004	*Me & Neesie*
Greenfield	Eloise & Jan Spivey Gilchrist	2006	*The Friendly Four*
Greenfield	Eloise & Jan Spivey Gilchrist	2006	*When the Horses Ride By: Children in the Times of War*
Greenfield	Eloise & Jerry Spivey Gilchrist	2008	*Brothers & Sisters: Family Poems*
Greenfield	Eloise & Jerry Pinkney	1994	*Mary McLeod Bethune*
Greenfield	Eloise & John Steptoe	1993	*She Come Bringing Me That Little Baby Girl*
Greenfield	Eloise & Leo and Diane Dillon	1986	*Honey, I Love and Other Love Poems*
Greenfield	Eloise & Moneta Barnett	1987	*Sister*
Greenfield	Eloise, Carole M. Byard Lessie Jones Little	1978	*I Can Do It by Myself*
Greenfield	Eloise, Gwendolyn Brooks, Norman Jordan, Langston Hughes, etc.	2003	*Make a Joyful Sound (poems for children by African American Poets)*
Greenfield	Eloise, Lessie Jones Little, and Jerry Pinkney	1993	*Childtimes: A Three-Generation Memoir*
Gremillion	Zachary P.		*AFRICAN ORIGINS OF FREEMASONRY: Treatise of the Ancient Grand Lodge of Khamet*
Grier	William H. & Price M. Cobbs	2000	*Black Rage*
Grimke	Charlotte Forten	1989	*The Journals of Charlotte Forten Grimke*

Hale	Janice E.	1994	*Unbank the Fire: Visions for the Education of African American Children*
Hale	Janice E., Walter Allen Bailey, and V.P. Franklin	2001	*Learning While Black: Creating Educational Excellence for African American Children*
Hale-Benson	Janice E.	1986	*Black Children: Their Roots, Culture, and Learning Styles*
Haley	Alex	1994	*Alex Haley's Queen*
Haley	Alex	1999	*Mama Flora's Family*
Haley	Alex	2000	*A Different Kind of Christmas*
Haley	Alex	2007	*Roots: The Saga of an American Family*
Hamilton	Virginia	1969	*The Time-Ago Tales of Jahdu*
Hamilton	Virginia	1983	*Sweet Whispers, Brother Rush*
Hamilton	Virginia	1990	*The Dark Way Stories from the Spirit World*
Hamilton	Virginia	1992	*Cousins*
Hamilton	Virginia	1992	*W.E.B. Dubois: A Biography*
Hamilton	Virginia	1993	*Anthony Burns: The Defeat and Triumph of a Fugitive Slave*
Hamilton	Virginia	1993	*Plain City*
Hamilton	Virginia	1995	*Arilla Sun Down*
Hamilton	Virginia	1997	*Mystery Of Drear House*
Hamilton	Virginia	1998	*Justice and Her Brothers*
Hamilton	Virginia	1998	*The Gathering*
Hamilton	Virginia	1999	*The Magical Adventures of Pretty Pearl*
Hamilton	Virginia	2000	*Second Cousins*
Hamilton	Virginia	2002	*Bluish*
Hamilton	Virginia	2005	*Time Pieces*
Hamilton	Virginia	2006	*The House of Dies Drear*
Hamilton	Virginia	2006	*The Planet of Junior Brown*
Hamilton	Virginia	2006	*M.C. Higgins, the Great*
Hamilton	Virginia	2006	*Zeely*
Hamilton	Virginia & Barry Moser	1991	*In the Beginning: Creation Stories from Around the World*
Hamilton	Virginia & Barry Moser	1991	*The All Jahdu Storybook*

Hamilton	Virginia & Barry Moser	1997	*A Ring of Tricksters : Animal Tales from America, the West Indies, And Africa*
Hamilton	Virginia & Barry Moser	2004	*Wee Winnie Witch's Skinny*
Hamilton	Virginia & Floyd Cooper	1997	*Jaguarundi*
Hamilton	Virginia & James Ransome	2003	*Bruh Rabbit And The Tar Baby Girl*
Hamilton	Virginia & Jerry Pinkney	1980	*Jahdu*
Hamilton	Virginia & Jerry Pinkney	1997	*Drylongso*
Hamilton	Virginia & Lambert Davis	1997	*The Bells of Christmas*
Hamilton	Virginia, Leo Dillon, and Diane Dillon	2000	*The Girl Who Spun Gold*
Hamilton	Virginia, Leo Dillon, and Diane Dillon	2002	*Many Thousand Gone: African Americans from Slavery to Freedom*
Hamilton	Virginia, Leo Dillon, and Diane Dillon	2004	*The People Could Fly: The Picture Book*
Hansberry	Lorraine	1994	*Les Blancs: The Collected Last Plays: The Drinking Gourd/What Use Are Flowers?*
Hansberry	Lorraine	1996	*To Be Young, Gifted and Black*
Hansberry	Lorraine	2004	*A Raisin in the Sun*
Hare	Nathan	1992	*Black Anglo-Saxons*
Hare	Nathan & Julia Hare	1984	*The Endangered Black Family: Coping With the Unisexualization and Coming Extinction of the Black Race*
Hare	Nathan & Julia Hare	1985	*Bringing the Black Boy to Manhood: The Passage*
Hare	Nathan & Julia Hare	1989	*Crisis in Black Sexual Politics*
Hare	Nathan & Julia Hare	1991	*The Miseducation of the Black Child -- The Hare Plan: Educate Every Black Man, Woman and Child*
Hare	Nathan & Julia Hare	2002	*The Black Agenda*
Hilliard	Asa G.	1987	*The Teachings of Ptahhotep: The Oldest Book in the World*
Hilliard	Asa G.	1987	*Testing African-American Students (Testing African American Students, Nos. 2, 3)*

Hilliard	Asa G.	1995	The Maroon Within Us: Selected Essays on African American Community Socialization
Hilliard	Asa G.	1998	SBA: The Reawakening of the African Mind
Hilliard	Asa G.	1998	African Power: Affirming African Indigenous Socialization in the Face of the Culture Wars
Hilliard	Asa G.	2005	EXCELLENCE IN EDUCATION VERSUS HIGH-STAKES STANDARDIZED TESTING.(Statistical Data Included): An article from: Journal of Teacher Education
Himes	Chester B.	1974	Black on Black; Baby sister and selected writings [by] Chester Himes
Himes	Chester B.	1988	The Real Cool Killers
Himes	Chester B.	1988	The Heat's On
Himes	Chester B.	1989	A Rage in Harlem
Himes	Chester B.	1989	The Crazy Kill
Himes	Chester B.	1989	Blind Man with a Pistol
Himes	Chester B.	1989	The Third Generation
Himes	Chester B.	1994	Cotton Comes to Harlem
Himes	Chester B.	1995	My Life of Absurdity: The Autobiography of Chester Himes
Himes	Chester B.	1995	The Quality of Hurt: The Early Years, the Autobiography of Chester Himes
Himes	Chester B.	1995	Run Man Run
Himes	Chester B.	1996	Pinktoes: A Novel
Himes	Chester B.	1997	Lonely Crusade
Himes	Chester B.	1999	Yesterday Will Make You Cry
Himes	Chester B.	2000	The Collected Stories of Chester Himes
Himes	Chester B.	2000	The End of a Primitive
Himes	Chester B.	2002	If He Hollers Let Him Go: A Novel
Himes	Chester B.	2007	All Shot Up: the classic crime thriller

Himes	Chester B.	2008	*The Big Gold Dream: The Classic Crime Thriller*
Hooks	Bell	1994	*Teaching to Transgress: Education as the Practice of Freedom*
Hooks	Bell	2003	*Teaching Community: A Pedagogy of Hope*
Hooks	Bell & Cornel West	1999	*Breaking Bread: Insurgent Black Intellectual Life*
Hopkinson	Nalo	1998	*Brown Girl in the Ring*
Hopkinson	Nalo	2000	*Midnight Robber*
Hopkinson	Nalo	2000	*Whispers from the Cotton Tree Root: Caribbean Fabulist Fiction*
Hopkinson	Nalo	2001	*Skin Folk*
Hopkinson	Nalo	2003	*Mojo: Conjure Stories*
Hopkinson	Nalo	2004	*The Salt Roads*
Hopkinson	Nalo	2007	*The New Moon's Arms*
Hopkinson	Nalo, Uppinder Mehan, and Samuel R. Delany	2004	*So Long Been Dreaming: Postcolonial Science Fiction & Fantasy*
Hughes	Langston		*Selected Poems of Langston Hughes*
Hughes	Langston		*Not Without Laughter*
Hughes	Langston		*The Langston Hughes Reader*
Hughes	Langston		*The Ways of White Folks: Stories*
Hughes	Langston		*I Wonder as I Wander: An Autobiographical Journey*
Hughes	Langston		*The Best of Simple*
Hughes	Langston		*Vintage Hughes*
Hughes	Langston		*Let America Be America Again: And Other Poems*
Hughes	Langston		*The Return of Simple*
Hughes	Langston & Arnold Rampersad		*The Big Sea: An Autobiography*
Hughes	Langston & Arnold Rampersad		*The Collected Poems of Langston Hughes*
Hughes	Langston & Arnold Rampersad		*The Poems: 1921-1940 (The Collected Works of Langston Hughes, Vol 1)*

Hughes	Langston & Brian Pinkney		The Dream Keeper and Other Poems
Hughes	Langston & Donna Akiba Sullivan Harper		Not So Simple: The "Simple" Stories
Hughes	Langston & Webster Smalley		Five Plays by Langston Hughes
Hughes	Langston, Carl Van Vechten, and Emily Bernard		Remember Me to Harlem: The Letters of Langston Hughes and Carl Van Vechten
Hughes	Langston, Romare Bearden, and Bill Cosby		The Block
Hurston	Zora Neale		Their Eyes Were Watching God
Hurston	Zora Neale		Every Tongue Got to Confess: Negro Folk-tales from the Gulf States
Hurston	Zora Neale		Dust Tracks on a Road: An Autobiography
Hurston	Zora Neale		I Love Myself When I Am Laughing... And Then Again: A Zora Neale Hurston Reader
Hurston	Zora Neale		Mules and Men
Hurston	Zora Neale		Tell My Horse: Voodoo and Life in Haiti and Jamaica
Hurston	Zora Neale		Jonah's Gourd Vine: A Novel
Hurston	Zora Neale		Seraph on the Suwanee: A Novel
Hurston	Zora Neale		Moses, Man of the Mountain
Hurston	Zora Neale		The Sanctified Church: The Folklore Writings of Zora Neale Hurston
Hurston	Zora Neale		Spunk: The Selected Stories of Zora Neale Hurston
Hurston	Zora Neale, Joyce Carol Thomas, and Bryan Collier		What's the Hurry, Fox?: And Other Animal Stories
Hurston	Zora Neale, Joyce Carol Thomas, and Christopher Myers		Lies and Other Tall Tales
Hurston	Zora Neale, Joyce Carol Thomas, and Leonard Jenkins		The Skull Talks Back: And Other Haunting Tales
Jackson	John G.	1971	Forgotten Thursdays
Jackson	John G.	1985	Christianity Before Christ
Jackson	John G.	1985	Ethiopia and the Origin of Civilization

Jackson	John G.	1987	*The Golden Ages of Africa*
Jackson	John G.	1987	*Hubert Henry Harrison: The Black Socrates*
Jackson	John G.	1987	*Was Jesus Christ a Negro*
Jackson	John G.	1987	*Black Reconstruction in South Carolina*
Jackson	John G.	1989	*Pagan Origins of the Christ Myth*
Jackson	John G.	1990	*Ages of Gold and Silver and Other Short Sketches of Human History*
Jackson	John G.	2001	*Introduction To African Civilizations*
Jackson	John G.	2001	*Man, God, and Civilization*
James	C. L. R.	1983	*Walter Rodney and the Question of Power*
James	C. L. R.	1989	*The Black Jacobins: Toussaint L'Ouverture and the San Domingo Revolution*
James	C. L. R.	1994	*C.L.R. James and revolutionary Marxism, selected writings of C.L.R. James1939-1949. Edited by Scott McLemee and Paul Le Blanc*
James	C. L. R. & Anna Grimshaw	1992	*The C.L.R. James Reader*
James	C. L. R. & David Austin	2009	*You Don't Play With Revolution: The Montréal Lectures of C.L.R. James*
James	C. L. R., Anna Grimshaw, and Keith Hart	1993	*American Civilization*
James	Cyril Lionel Robert	1968	*C.L.R. James on the origins; in Radical America: Vol. II, No. 4, July-August, 1968*
James	George G. M.		*STOLEN LEGACY*
Jones	Gayl	1987	*Corregidora*
Jones	Gayl	1987	*Eva's Man*
Jones	Gayl	1991	*Liberating Voices: Oral Tradition in African American Literature*
Jones	Gayl	1999	*The Healing*
Jones	Gayl	2000	*Mosquito*
Jones	Gayl	2000	*Song for Anniho*
Jones	Gayl	2005	*White Rat: Stories*

Jordan	June	1985	*On Call*
Jordan	June	1989	*Naming Our Destiny: New and Selected Poems*
Jordan	June	1993	*Haruko/Love Poems*
Jordan	June	1993	*Living Room*
Jordan	June	1995	*June Jordan's Poetry for the People: A Revolutionary Blueprint*
Jordan	June	1995	*Civil Wars*
Jordan	June	1995	*I Was Looking at the Ceiling and Then I Saw the Sky*
Jordan	June	1997	*Kissing God Goodbye: Poems 1991-1997*
Jordan	June	1998	*Affirmative Acts*
Jordan	June	2001	*Soldier: A Poet's Childhood*
Jordan	June	2004	*Soulscript: A Collection of Classic African American Poetry*
Jordan	June	2007	*Directed by Desire: The Collected Poems of June Jordan*
Jordan	June	2008	*Some of Us Did Not Die: New and Selected Essays*
Jordan	June & Terri Bush	1970	*Voice of the Children*
King	Richard	2001	*African Origin of Biological Psychiatry*
King	Richard	2001	*Melanin: A Key To Freedom*
Kunjufu	Jawanza	1984	*Developing Positive Self-Images & Discipline in Black Children*
Kunjufu	Jawanza	1987	*Lessons from History, Elementary Edition: A Celebration in Blackness*
Kunjufu	Jawanza	1989	*Critical Issues in Educating African American Youth (A Talk With Jawanza)*
Kunjufu	Jawanza	1993	*Hip-Hop vs MAAT : A Psycho/Social Analysis of Values*

Kunjufu	Jawanza	1997	*Motivating and Preparing Black Youth for Success*
Kunjufu	Jawanza	1997	*To Be Popular or Smart: The Black Peer Group*
Kunjufu	Jawanza	1997	*Restoring the Village, Values, and Commitment: Solutions for the Black Family*
Kunjufu	Jawanza	1997	*Adam! Where Are You?: Why Most Black Men Don't Go to Church*
Kunjufu	Jawanza	1997	*The Power, Passion & Pain of Black Love*
Kunjufu	Jawanza	1998	*Black College Student Survival Guide*
Kunjufu	Jawanza	1999	*Sankofa: Stories of Power, Hope, and Joy*
Kunjufu	Jawanza	2000	*Satan, I'm Taking Back My Health!*
Kunjufu	Jawanza	2002	*Black Students / Middle Class Teachers*
Kunjufu	Jawanza	2002	*Black Economics: Solutions for Economic and Community Empowerment*
Kunjufu	Jawanza	2002	*Good Brothers Looking for Good Sisters*
Kunjufu	Jawanza	2004	*Countering the Conspiracy to Destroy Black Boys (Series) (v. 1-4)*
Kunjufu	Jawanza	2004	*Solutions for Black America*
Kunjufu	Jawanza	2005	*Hip Hop Street Curriculum*
Kunjufu	Jawanza	2005	*Keeping Black Boys Out of Special Education*
Kunjufu	Jawanza	2006	*Developing Strong Black Male Ministries*
Kunjufu	Jawanza	2007	*An African Centered Response to Ruby Payne's Poverty Theory*
Kunjufu	Jawanza	2007	*Raising Black Boys*
Kunjufu	Jawanza	2007	*A Culture of Respect*

Kunjufu	Jawanza	2008	*100+ Educational Strategies to Teach Children of Color*
Kunjufu	Jawanza	2009	*State of Emergency*
Kunjufu	Jawanza & Folami Prescott	2003	*SETCLAE, High School: Self-Esteem Through Culture Leads to Academic Excellence*
Kunjufu	Jawanza & Lady June Hubbard	1997	*Up Against the Wall*
Kunjufu	Jawanza, Erica Myles, and Nichelle Wilson	1999	*Great Negroes: Past and Present: Volume Two*
Kuykendall	Crystal	1976	*Developing leadership for parent/ citizen groups*
Kuykendall	Crystal	1989	*Improving black student achievement by enhancing students' self-image (Mid-Atlantic Equity Center series)*
Kuykendall	Crystal	2004	*From Rage to Hope: Strategies for Reclaiming Black & Hispanic Students*
Ladson-Billings	Gloria	2009	*The Dreamkeepers: Successful Teachers of African American Children*
Lincoln	C. Eric	1964	*My face is black*
Lincoln	C. Eric	1966	*Coming through the fire; surviving race and place in America*
Lincoln	C. Eric	1968	*SOUNDS OF THE STRUGGLE*
Lincoln	C. Eric	1969	*Negro Pilgrimage in America : Coming of Age of the Black Americans*
Lincoln	C. Eric	1974	*The Black experience in religion*
Lincoln	C. Eric	1985	*Martin Luther King, Jr.*
Lincoln	C. Eric	1988	*Avenue (The), Clayton City, A Novel*
Lincoln	C. Eric	1990	*This Road Since Freedom: Collected Poems*
Lincoln	C. Eric	1994	*The Black Muslims in America*

Lincoln	C. Eric	1999	*Race, Religion, and the Continuing American Dilemma*
Lincoln	C. Eric & Lawrence Mamiya	1990	*The Black Church in the African American Experience*
Locke	Alain Leroy	1969	*The Negro and His Music; Negro Art: Past and Present*
Locke	Alain Leroy	1992	*Race Contacts and Interracial Relations: Lectures on the Theory and Practice of Race*
Locke	Alain Leroy	1999	*The New Negro : Voices of the Harlem Renaissance*
Loewen	James W.	1988	*The Mississippi Chinese : Between Black and White*
Loewen	James W.	1988	*Gender bias in SAT items (SuDoc ED 1.310/2:294915)*
Loewen	James W.	1992	*Lies My Teacher Told Me About Christopher Columbus: What Your History Books Got Wrong*
Loewen	James W.	2006	*Sundown Towns: A Hidden Dimension of American Racism*
Loewen	James W.	2007	*Lies Across America: What American Historic Sites Get Wrong*
Loewen	James W.	2008	*Lies My Teacher Told Me: Everything Your American History Textbook Got Wrong, Revised and Updated Edition*
Lorde	Audre	1983	*Zami: A New Spelling of My Name*
Lorde	Audre	2000	*The Collected Poems of Audre Lorde*
Lorde	Audre	2000	*The Uses of the Erotic: The Erotic as Power*
Lorde	Audre	2007	*Sister Outsider: Essays and Speeches*
Maathai	Wangari	2003	*The Green Belt Movement: Sharing the Approach and the Experience*

Maathai	Wangari	2007	*Unbowed: A Memoir*
Maathai	Wangari	2009	*The Challenge for Africa*
Madhubuti	Haki R.	1972	*Kwanzaa; an African-Amerian holiday that is progressive and uplifting*
Madhubuti	Haki R.	1973	*From Plan to Planet*
Madhubuti	Haki R.	1978	*Enemies: The Clash of Races*
Madhubuti	Haki R.	1983	*Earthquakes and Sun Rise Missions: Poetry and Essays of Black Renewal 1973-1983*
Madhubuti	Haki R.	1987	*Killing Memory, Seeking Ancestors*
Madhubuti	Haki R.	1991	*Black Men, Obsolete, Single, Dangerous?: The Afrikan American Family in Transition*
Madhubuti	Haki R.	1992	*Don't Cry, Scream*
Madhubuti	Haki R.	1993	*Why L.A. Happened: Implications of the '92 Los Angeles Rebellion*
Madhubuti	Haki R.	1995	*Claiming Earth: Race, Rage, Rape, Redemption: Blacks Seeking a Culture of Enlightened Empowerment*
Madhubuti	Haki R.	1998	*HeartLove: Wedding and Love Poems*
Madhubuti	Haki R.	2002	*Tough Notes: A Healing Call for Creating Exceptional Black Men*
Madhubuti	Haki R.	2004	*Run Toward Fear: New Poems and a Poet's Handbook*
Madhubuti	Haki R.	2006	*YellowBlack: The First Twenty-One Years of a Poet's Life*
Madhubuti	Haki R. & Safisha L. Madhubuti	2009	*African-Centered Education: Its Value, Importance, and Necessity in the Development of Black Children*
Madhubuti	Haki R.	2009	*Liberation Narratives: New and Collected Poems, 1966 - 2009*
Mandela	Nelson	1996	*Mandela: An Illustrated Autobiography*

Mandela	Nelson	2000	*Long Walk to Freedom: The Autobiography of Nelson Mandela : With Connections*
Mandela	Nelson	2007	*Nelson Mandela's Favorite African Folktales*
Mandela	Nelson & Bill Clinton	2004	*In His Own Words*
Maplethorpe	Robert	1986	*THE BLACK BOOK*
Marable	Manning		*How Capitalism Underdeveloped Black America: Problems in Race, Political Economy, and Society*
Marable	Manning		*Race, Class and Democracy: Walter Rodney's Thought on the Black American Struggle*
Marshall	Paule	1984	*Praisesong for the Widow*
Marshall	Paule	1984	*The Chosen Place, The Timeless People*
Marshall	Paule	1988	*Soul Clap Hands and Sing*
Marshall	Paule	1993	*Reena and Other Stories: Including the Novella "Merle"*
Marshall	Paule	2001	*The Fisher King: A Novel*
Marshall	Paule	2004	*Daughters*
Marshall	Paule	2009	*Brown Girl, Brownstones*
Marshall	Paule	2009	*Triangular Road: A Memoir*
Martin	Tony	1983	*Marcus Garvey, Hero: A First Biography*
Martin	Tony	1983	*Literary Garveyism: Garvey, Black Arts, and the Harlem Renaissance*
Martin	Tony	1986	*Race First: The Ideological and Organizational Struggles of Marcus Garvey and the Universal Negro Improvement Association*
Martin	Tony	1986	*African Fundamentalism: A Literary Anthology of the Garvey Movement*

Martin	Tony	1998	Pan-African Connection: From Slavery to Garvey and Beyond
Martin	Tony	2000	Amy Ashwood Garvey: Pan-Africanist, Feminist, and Wife No. 1
May	Nathaniel, Clint Willis, and James W. Loewen	2003	We Are the People: Voices from the Other Side of American History
Mays	Benjamin Elijah	1983	Quotable Quotes of Benjamin E. Mays
Mays	Benjamin Elijah	2003	Born to Rebel: An Autobiography
Meier	August & John Hope Franklin		Black Leaders of the Twentieth Century (Blacks in the New World)
Morrison	Toni	1987	Tar Baby
Morrison	Toni	1993	Playing in the Dark: Whiteness and the Literary Imagination
Morrison	Toni	1993	The Bluest Eye
Morrison	Toni	1999	Paradise
Morrison	Toni	2004	Remember: The Journey to School Integration
Morrison	Toni	2004	Sula
Morrison	Toni	2004	Jazz
Morrison	Toni	2004	Song of Solomon
Morrison	Toni	2004	Beloved
Morrison	Toni	2005	Love: A Novel
Morrison	Toni	2008	What Moves at the Margin: Selected Nonfiction
Morrison	Toni	2008	A Mercy
Morrison	Toni & Slade Morrison	2002	Book of Mean People, The
Morrison	Toni & Slade Morrison	2002	The Big Box
Moses	Robert, Theresa Perry, Ernesto Cortes, & Lisa Delpit	2008	Quality Education as a Civil Right: Creating Grassroots Movement to Transform Public Schools
Mosley	Walter	1996	R L's Dream
Mosley	Walter	1998	Always Outnumbered, Always Outgunned

Mosley	Walter	1998	*Blue Light*
Mosley	Walter	2000	*Walkin' the Dog*
Mosley	Walter	2002	*Devil in a Blue Dress*
Mosley	Walter	2002	*Fearless Jones*
Mosley	Walter	2002	*Gone Fishin': Featuring an Original Easy Rawlins Short Story "Smoke"*
Mosley	Walter	2002	*White Butterfly*
Mosley	Walter	2002	*A Red Death*
Mosley	Walter	2002	*Black Betty*
Mosley	Walter	2002	*A Little Yellow Dog*
Mosley	Walter	2002	*Futureland*
Mosley	Walter	2003	*Six Easy Pieces: Easy Rawlins Stories*
Mosley	Walter	2003	*What Next: A Memoir Toward World Peace*
Mosley	Walter	2005	*The Man in My Basement: A Novel*
Mosley	Walter	2005	*Life Out of Context*
Mosley	Walter	2006	*47*
Mosley	Walter	2006	*Workin' on the Chain Gang*
Mosley	Walter	2007	*Fear of the Dark: A Novel*
Mosley	Walter	2007	*Fortunate Son: A Novel*
Mosley	Walter	2007	*The Wave*
Mosley	Walter	2008	*The Right Mistake: The Further Philosophical Investigations of Socrates Fortlow*
Mosley	Walter	2008	*Blonde Faith*
Mosley	Walter	2008	*Diablerie: A Novel*
Mosley	Walter	2008	*Killing Johnny Fry: A Sexistential Novel*
Mosley	Walter	2008	*Cinnamon Kiss: A Novel*
Mosley	Walter	2008	*Little Scarlet*
Mosley	Walter	2008	*Bad Boy Brawly Brown*
Mosley	Walter	2009	*The Long Fall*
Mosley	Walter	2009	*The Tempest Tales: A Novel-in-Stories*
Mosley	Walter	2009	*This Year You Write Your Novel*

Nascimento	Abdias do	1976	*Genocide--the social lynching of the black in Brazil*
Nascimento	Abdias do	1977	*Racial democracy in Brazil, myth or reality ?: A dossier of Brazilian racism*
Nascimento	Abdias do	1977	*Orixas*
Nascimento	Abdias do	1978	*Black Mystery*
Nascimento	Abdias do & Elisa Larkin Nascimento	1989	*Brazil, Mixture or Massacre?: Essays in the Genocide of a Black People*
Nascimento	Abdias do & Elisa Larkin Nascimento	1992	*Africans in Brazil: A Pan-African Perspective*
Nascimento	Abdias do & Peter Lownds	1978	*Sortilege (Black Mystery)*
Nascimento	Elisa Larkin	2006	*The Sorcery of Color: Identity, Race, and Gender in Brazil*
Neville	Dr. Helen A., Dr. Brendesha M. Tynes, and Dr. Shawn O. Utsey		*Handbook of African American Psychology*
Nkrumah	Kwame	1965	*Neo-Colonialism: The Last Stage of Imperialism*
Nkrumah	Kwame	1970	*Consciencism: Philosophy and the Ideology for Decolonization*
Nkrumah	Kwame	1973	*Revolutionary Path*
Nkrumah	Kwame	1989	*Ghana: Autobiography of Kwame Nkrumah*
Nkrumah	Kwame	2006	*AFRICA MUST UNITE*
Nkrumah	Kwame	2006	*Class Struggle In Africa*
Nkrumah	Kwame	2006	*VOICE FROM CONAKRY*
Nkrumah	Kwame	2006	*THE STRUGGLE CONTINUES*
Ogbu	John U.	1974	*Next Generation*
Ogbu	John U.	1978	*Minority Education and Caste: The American System in Cross-Cultural Perspective*
Ogbu	John U.	2003	*Black American Students in An Affluent Suburb: A Study of Academic Disengagement*
Ogbu	John U.	2008	*Minority Status, Oppositional Culture and Schooling*
Ogbu	John U. & Margaret A. Gibson	1991	*Minority Status and Schooling: A Comparative Study of Immigrant and Involuntary Minorities*

Ogbu	John U. & R. Patrick Soloman	1992	*Black Resistance in High School: Forging a Separatist Culture*
Outlaw	Lucius T.	1989	*Philosophy, ethnicity, and race*
Outlaw	Lucius T.	1996	*On Race and Philosophy*
Outlaw	Lucius T.	2005	*Critical Social Theory in the Interests of Black Folks*
Padmore	George	1953	*The Gold Coast Revolution - The Struggle of an African People from Slavery to Freedom*
Padmore	George	1969	*Africa: Britain's third empire*
Padmore	George	1971	*The life and struggles of Negro toilers*
Padmore	George	1972	*Pan-Africanism or Communism*
Padmore	George		*Africa and World Peace*
Payne-Jackson	Arvilla and John Lee		*Folk Wisdom and Mother Wit: John Lee--An African American Herbal Healer*
Perry	Theresa & Lisa D. Delpit	2008	*The Real Ebonics Debate: Power, Language, and the Education of African-american Children*
Reed	Ishmael	1972	*Conjure; Selected Poems, 1963-1970*
Reed	Ishmael	1996	*Mumbo Jumbo*
Reed	Ishmael	1996	*Japanese by Spring*
Reed	Ishmael	1998	*Flight to Canada*
Reed	Ishmael	1998	*Multi-America: Essays on Cultural Wars and Cultural Peace*
Reed	Ishmael	1999	*The Freelance Pallbearers*
Reed	Ishmael	1999	*The Terrible Twos*
Reed	Ishmael	2000	*Yellow Back Radio Broke-Down*
Reed	Ishmael	2000	*Reckless Eyeballing*
Reed	Ishmael	2000	*The Last Days of Louisiana Red*
Reed	Ishmael	2001	*The Reed Reader*

Reed	Ishmael	2003	*Blues City: A Walk in Oakland*
Reed	Ishmael	2004	*Another Day At The Front: Dispatches From The Race War*
Reed	Ishmael	2007	*New and Collected Poems 1964-2007*
Reed	Ishmael	2008	*Mixing It Up: Taking On the Media Bullies and Other Reflections*
Reed	Ishmael & Carla Blank	2009	*Pow-Wow: Charting the Fault Lines in the American Experience - Short Fiction from Then to Now*
Reed	Ishmael, Franklin Sirmans, Robert Farris Thompson, and Jen Budney	2008	*NeoHooDoo: Art for a Forgotten Faith*
Robeson	Paul	1998	*Here I Stand*
Robeson	Paul	1998	*Paul Robeson Speaks: Writings, Speeches, and Interviews, a Centennial Celebration*
Robeson	Paul	2003	*Paul Robeson: The Journey of a Renaissance Man*
Rodney	Walter	1967	*West Africa and the Atlantic slave-trade*
Rodney	Walter	1968	*BLACK POWERITS RELEVANCE TO THE WEST INDIES (WALTER RODNEY, 1968)*
Rodney	Walter	1981	*How Europe Underdeveloped Africa*
Rodney	Walter	1981	*A History of the Guyanese Working People, 1881-1905*
Rodney	Walter	1983	*The Groundings With My Brothers*
Rodney	Walter	1990	*Walter Rodney Speaks: The Making of an African Intellectual*
Rodney	Walter	2008	*A History of the Upper Guinea Coast, 1545-1800*
Rogers	Joel Augustus	1957	*From Superman to Man*

122   APPENDIX 1

Rogers	Joel Augustus	1960	*World's Great Men of Color, Volume I: Asia and Africa, and Historical Figures Before Christ, Including Aesop, Hannibal, Cleopatra, Zenobia, Askia the Great, and Many Others*
Rogers	Joel Augustus	1961	*Africa's Gift to America: The Afro-American in the Making and Saving of the United States : With New Supplement, Africa and Its Potentialities by J. A. Rogers (Hardcover - Jun 1961)*
Rogers	Joel Augustus	1965	*The Five Negro Presidents: According to what White People Said They Were*
Rogers	Joel Augustus	1967	*Sex and Race: A History of White, Negro, and Indian Miscegenation in the Two Americas : The New World*
Rogers	Joel Augustus	1970	*Sex and Race: Negro-Caucasian Mixing in All Ages and All Lands : The Old World*
Rogers	Joel Augustus	1972	*Sex and Race, Vol. 3: Why White and Black Mix in Spite of Opposition*
Rogers	Joel Augustus	1980	*100 Amazing Facts About the Negro With Complete Proof: A Short Cut to the World History of the Negro*
Rogers	Joel Augustus	1980	*Nature Knows No Color-Line: Research into the Negro Ancestry in the White Race*
Rogers	Joel Augustus	1980	*Ku Klux Spirit*
Rogers	Joel Augustus	1982	*The Real Facts About Ethiopia (B.C.P. Pamphlet)*
Rogers	Joel Augustus	1983	*Your History: From Beginning of Time to the Present*
Said	Edward W.	1979	*Orientalism*
Said	Edward W.	1983	*The World, the Text, and the Critic*

Said	Edward W.	1992	*The Question of Palestine*
Said	Edward W.	1994	*Culture and Imperialism*
Said	Edward W.	1997	*Covering Islam: How the Media and the Experts Determine How We See the Rest of the World*
Said	Edward W.	2000	*Out of Place: A Memoir*
Said	Edward W.	2002	*Power, Politics, and Culture*
Said	Edward W.	2002	*Reflections on Exile and Other Essays (Convergences: Inventories of the Present)*
Sanchez	Sonia	1969	*Home Coming*
Sanchez	Sonia	1971	*Ima talken bout The Nation of Islam*
Sanchez	Sonia	1973	*A Blues Book for Blue Black Magical Women*
Sanchez	Sonia	1975	*Love Poems*
Sanchez	Sonia	1982	*We a Baddddd People*
Sanchez	Sonia	1983	*It's a new day; (poems for young brothas and sistuhs)*
Sanchez	Sonia	1985	*I've Been a Woman: New and Selected Poems*
Sanchez	Sonia	1985	*A Sound Investment, Stories By Sonia Sanchez*
Sanchez	Sonia	1986	*Generations: Selected Poetry, 1969-1985*
Sanchez	Sonia	1987	*Under a Soprano Sky*
Sanchez	Sonia	1997	*Wounded in the House of a Friend*
Sanchez	Sonia	1998	*Does Your House Have Lions ?*
Sanchez	Sonia	1999	*Like the Singing Coming Off the Drums*
Sanchez	Sonia	2000	*Shake Loose My Skin: New and Selected Poems*
Sanchez	Sonia	2007	*Homegirls and Handgrenades*
Shange	Ntzake	1991	*Nappy Edges*
Shange	Ntzake	1992	*Three Pieces*
Shange	Ntzake	1995	*Betsey Brown: A Novel*

Shange	Ntzake	1995	*Liliane: A Novel*
Shange	Ntzake	1997	*For Colored Girls Who Have Considered Suicide When the Rainbow Is Enuf*
Shange	Ntzake	1999	*If I Can Cook/You Know God Can*
Shange	Ntzake	2003	*Daddy Says*
Shange	Ntzake	19960	*Sassafrass, Cypress and Indigo: A Novel*
Shange	Ntzake & Ifa Bayeza	2009	*How I Come by This Cryin' Song*
Shange	Ntzake & Kadir Nelson	2004	*Ellington Was Not a Street*
Shange	Ntzake & Kadir Nelson	2009	*Coretta Scott*
Shange	Ntzake & Michael Sporn	1997	*Whitewash*
Shange	Ntzake, Romare Bearden, Eric Baker, and Linda Sunshine	1994	*I Live In Music*
Shor	Ira & Paulo Freire	1986	*A Pedagogy for Liberation: Dialogues on Transforming Education*
Smith	Charles H. & Cain Hope Felder	2001	*African American Jubilee Legacy- Spiritual Odyssey*
Some	Malidoma Patrice	1995	*Of Water and the Spirit: Ritual, Magic and Initiation in the Life of an African Shaman*
Some	Malidoma Patrice	1997	*Ritual: Power, Healing and Community*
Some	Malidoma Patrice	1999	*The Healing Wisdom of Africa*
Soyinka	Wole	1965	*The Road (Three Crowns)*
Soyinka	Wole	1966	*The Lion and the Jewel*
Soyinka	Wole	1973	*Collected Plays: Volume 1*
Soyinka	Wole	1975	*Collected Plays 2*
Soyinka	Wole	1984	*A Play of Giants*
Soyinka	Wole	1987	*Death and the King's Horseman*
Soyinka	Wole	1988	*The Man Died: The Prison Notes of Wole Soyinka*
Soyinka	Wole	1989	*Ake: The Years of Childhood*

Soyinka	Wole	1994	ART, DIALOGUE, AND OUTRAGE: Essays on Literature and Culture
Soyinka	Wole	1996	Interpreters
Soyinka	Wole	1997	The Open Sore of a Continent: A Personal Narrative of the Nigerian Crisis
Soyinka	Wole	1998	Early Poems
Soyinka	Wole	1999	Soyinka Plays: Play of Giants; From Zia with Love; A Source of Hyacinths; The Beatification of Area Boy v. 2
Soyinka	Wole	2000	The Burden of Memory, the Muse of Forgiveness
Soyinka	Wole	2002	Selected Poems: A Shuttle in the Crypt, Idanre, Mandela's Earth
Soyinka	Wole	2004	The Bacchae of Euripides: A Communion Rite
Soyinka	Wole	2005	Climate of Fear: The Quest for Dignity in a Dehumanized World
Soyinka	Wole	2007	You Must Set Forth at Dawn: A Memoir
Soyinka	Wole	2007	Ibadan: The Penkelemes Years - A Memoir, 1945-67
Soyinka	Wole	2008	Myth, Literature and the African World
Soyinka	Wole & Simon Gikandi	2002	Death and the King's Horseman
Stuckey	Sterling	1972	The ideological origins of Black nationalism
Stuckey	Sterling	1988	Slave Culture: Nationalist Theory and the Foundations of Black America
Stuckey	Sterling	1994	Going Through the Storm: The Influence of African American Art in History
Stuckey	Sterling & Linda kerrigan Salvucci	1999	Call to Freedom: Beginnings to 1877
Sudakarsa	Niara	1973	Where Women Work A Study of Yoruba Women in the Marketplace and in the Home

Sudakarsa	Niara	1989	*Can we afford equity and excellence? Can we afford less?*
Sudakarsa	Niara	1989	*Racial and cultural diversity is a key part of the pursuit of excellence in the University and Affirmative action or affirmation of the status quo?*
Sudakarsa	Niara	1995	*The Barnes Bond Connection*
Sudakarsa	Niara	1996	*Exploring the African-American Experience*
Sudakarsa	Niara	1997	*The Strength of Our Mothers: African & African American Women & Families : Essays and Speeches*
Sudakarsa	Niara	1998	*Education Is Still the Key: Selected Speeches & Essays*
Tatum	Beverly Daniel	2003	*"Why Are All The Black Kids Sitting Together in the Cafeteria?": A Psychologist Explains the Development of Racial Identity*
Thiong'o	Ngugi wa	1986	*Decolonising the Mind: The Politics of Language in African Literature*
Thiong'o	Ngugi wa	1993	*Moving the Centre: The Struggle for Cultural Freedoms*
Thiong'o	Ngugi wa	2009	*Something Torn and New: An African Renaissance*
Thurman	Howard	1963	*Disciplines of the Spirit*
Thurman	Howard	1965	*The Luminous Darkness: A Personal Interpretation of the Anatomy of Segregation and the Ground of Hope*
Thurman	Howard	1972	*The Creative Encounter*
Thurman	Howard	1974	*Growing Edge*

Thurman	Howard	1975	*Deep River and The Negro Spiritual Speaks of Life and Death*
Thurman	Howard	1978	*Temptations of Jesus*
Thurman	Howard	1978	*Deep Is the Hunger*
Thurman	Howard	1981	*With Head and Heart: The Autobiography of Howard Thurman*
Thurman	Howard	1984	*The Centering Moment*
Thurman	Howard	1984	*For the Inward Journey*
Thurman	Howard	1985	*The Mood of Christmas*
Thurman	Howard	1986	*The Search for Common Ground*
Thurman	Howard	1989	*The Luminous Darkness: A Personal Interpretation of the Anatomy of Segregation and the Ground of Hope*
Thurman	Howard	1996	*Jesus and the Disinherited*
Thurman	Howard	1999	*A Strange Freedom*
Thurman	Howard	1999	*Meditations of the Heart*
Thurman	Howard	2003	*Howard Thurman: Essential Writings*
Thurman	Howard	2007	*The Inward Journey*
Toure	Ahmed Sekou	1979	*Africa on the Move*
Van Sertima	Ivan	1968	*CARIBBEAN WRITERS: CRITICAL ESSAYS*
Van Sertima	Ivan	1983	*Blacks in Science: Ancient and Modern*
Van Sertima	Ivan	1986	*African Presence in Early Europe*
Van Sertima	Ivan	1987	*African Presence in Early America*
Van Sertima	Ivan	1988	*Black Women in Antiquity*
Van Sertima	Ivan	1988	*Great Black Leaders: Ancient and Modern*
Van Sertima	Ivan	1989	*Egypt Revisited*
Van Sertima	Ivan	1991	*The Golden Age of the Moor*
Van Sertima	Ivan	1995	*Egypt: Child of Africa*
Van Sertima	Ivan	1998	*Early America Revisited*

Van Sertima	Ivan	2003	*They Came Before Columbus: The African Presence in Ancient America*
Van Sertima	Ivan & Larry Williams	1986	*Great African Thinkers: Cheikh Anta Diop*
Van Sertima	Ivan & Ronoko Rashidi	1987	*African Presence in Early Asia*
Van Sertima	Ivan & Wayne Chandler	1998	*Ancient Future*
Walcott	Derek	1971	*Dream on Monkey Mountain and Other Plays*
Walcott	Derek	1980	*Remembrance and Pantomime: Two Plays*
Walcott	Derek	1984	*Midsummer*
Walcott	Derek	1987	*Collected Poems, 1948-1984*
Walcott	Derek	1988	*The Arkansas Testament*
Walcott	Derek	1998	*The Bounty: Poems*
Walcott	Derek	1999	*What the Twilight Says: Essays*
Walcott	Derek	2001	*Tiepolo's Hound*
Walcott	Derek	2002	*Omeros*
Walcott	Derek	2002	*Walker and The Ghost Dance: Plays*
Walcott	Derek	2002	*The Haitian Trilogy: Plays: Henri Christophe, Drums and Colours, and The Haytian Earth*
Walcott	Derek	2006	*The Prodigal: A Poem*
Walcott	Derek	2007	*Selected Poems*
Walcott	Derek & Homer	1993	*The Odyssey: A Stage Version*
Walker	Alice	1973	*Revolutionary Petunias*
Walker	Alice	1976	*Once*
Walker	Alice	1989	*Living by the Word*
Walker	Alice	1990	*The Temple of My Familiar*
Walker	Alice	1991	*Finding the Green Stone*
Walker	Alice	1992	*The Same River Twice*
Walker	Alice	1993	*To Hell with Dying*
Walker	Alice	1994	*Everyday Use*
Walker	Alice	1996	*Alice Walker Banned*

Walker	Alice	1998	*Anything We Love Can Be Saved*
Walker	Alice	1999	*By the Light of My Father's Smile: A Novel*
Walker	Alice	2001	*The Way Forward Is with a Broken Heart*
Walker	Alice	2003	*A Poem Traveled Down My Arm: Poems and Drawings*
Walker	Alice	2003	*Her Blue Body Everything We Know: Earthling Poems 1965-1990 Complete*
Walker	Alice	2003	*The Third Life of Grange Copeland*
Walker	Alice	2003	*In Love & Trouble: Stories of Black Women*
Walker	Alice	2003	*Meridian*
Walker	Alice	2003	*In Search of Our Mother's Garden*
Walker	Alice	2004	*Absolute Trust in the Goodness of the Earth: New Poems*
Walker	Alice	2005	*Now Is the Time to Open Your Heart: A Novel*
Walker	Alice	2006	*The Color Purple*
Walker	Alice	2006	*There Is a Flower at the Tip of My Nose Smelling Me*
Walker	Alice	2006	*We Are the Ones We Have Been Waiting For: Light in a Time of Darkness*
Walker	Alice	2007	*Why War Is Never a Good Idea*
Walker	Alice	2008	*Possessing the Secret of Joy: A Novel*
Walker	Margaret	1968	*For My People*
Walker	Margaret	1989	*This Is My Century: New and Collected Poems*
Walker	Margaret	1999	*Jubilee*
Washington	Booker Taliferio	1992	*Booker T. Washington The Negro in Business*

Washington	Booker Taliferio	1995	*Black Diamonds: The Wisdom of Booker T. Washington*
Washington	Booker Taliferio	2007	*Working With The Hands: Being A Sequel To Up From Slavery Covering The Author's Experiences In Industrial Training At Tuskegee*
Washington	Booker Taliferio	2008	*Character Building*
Washington	Booker Taliferio	2008	*The Negro Problem*
Washington	Booker Taliferio	2008	*My Larger Education*
Washington	Booker Taliferio	2009	*Up from Slavery - An Autobiography*
Welsing	Frances Cress	1990	*The Cress Theory of Color-Confrontation and Racism (White Supremacy) (A Psycho-Genetic Theory and World Outlook)*
Welsing	Frances Cress	2004	*The Isis Papers: The Keys to the Colors*
West	Cornel	1989	*The American Evasion of Philosophy: A Genealogy of Pragmatism*
West	Cornel	1991	*The Ethical Dimensions of Marxist Thought*
West	Cornel	1993	*Prophetic Thought in Postmodern Times*
West	Cornel	1993	*Prophetic Fragments: Illuminations of the Crisis in American Religion and Culture*
West	Cornel	1999	*Restoring Hope*
West	Cornel	2001	*Race Matters*
West	Cornel	2002	*Prophesy Deliverance!*
West	Cornel	2004	*Democracy Matters: Winning the Fight Against Imperialism*
West	Cornel	2008	*Hope on a Tightrope: Words and Wisdom*

West	Cornel	2008	*Keeping Faith: Philosophy and Race in America*
West	Cornel & Eddie S. Glaude Jr.	2003	*African American Religious Thought: An Anthology*
Wiggins	Lida Keck & William Dean Howells	2007	*The Life And Works Of Paul Laurence Dunbar: Containing His Complete Poetical Works, His Best Short Stories, Numerous Anecdotes And A Complete Biography Of The Famous Poet*
Williams	Chancellor		*The Destruction of Black Civilization*
Williams	Larry O., Asa G., III Hilliard, and Lucretia Payton-Stewart	1996	*Infusion of African & African American Content in the School Curriculum*
Wilson	Amos N.	1978	*Developmental Psychology of the Black Child*
Wilson	Amos N.	1989	*Letters from India*
Wilson	Amos N.	1991	*Black-On-Black Violence: The Psychodynamics of Black Self-Annihilation in Service of White Domination*
Wilson	Amos N.	1992	*Awakening the Natural Genius of Black Children*
Wilson	Amos N.	1992	*Understanding Black Adolescent Male Violence: Its Remediation and Prevention*
Wilson	Amos N.	1993	*The Falsification of Afrikan Consciousness: Eurocentric History, Psychiatry and the Politics of White Supremacy*
Wilson	Amos N.	1998	*Blueprint for Black Power: A Moral, Political, and Economic Imperative for the Twenty-First Century*

Wilson	Amos N.	1999	Afrikan-centered consciousness versus the new world order: Garveyism in the age of globalism
Woodson	Carter G.	1922	The Negro In Our History
Woodson	Carter G.	1925	Free Negro heads of families in the United States in 1830: Together with a brief treatment of the free Negro
Woodson	Carter G.	2000	The Mis-education of the Negro
Woodson	Carter G.	2008	A Century of Negro Migration
Woodson	Carter G.		The Education Of The Negro Prior To 1861: A History Of The Education Of The Colored People Of The United States From The Beginning Of Slavery To The Civil War
Woodson	Carter G.		Negro Makers of History
Wright	Bobby E.	1985	Psychopathic Racial Personality and Other Essays
Wright	Richard	1940	Native Son
Wright	Richard	2003	Clara Callan: A Novel
Wright	Richard		Black Boy
Wright	Richard		A Father's Law
Wright	Richard		Uncle Tom's Children
Wright	Richard		The Outsider
Wright	Richard		Eight Men: Short Stories
Wright	Richard		Black Power: Three Books from Exile: Black Power; The Color Curtain; and White Man, Listen!
Wright	Richard & David Diaz	1995	Rite of Passage

Wright	Richard, United States Farm Security Administration, Edwin Rosskam, and David Bradley	2002	*12 Million Black Voices*
X	Malcolm Malcolm & Alex Haley	1992	*By Any Means Necessary*
X	Malcolm &	1973	*The Autobiography of Malcolm X*
X	Bruce Perry	1989	*Malcolm X: The Last Speeches*
Zaslavsky	Claudia	1982	*Tic Tac Toe: And Other Three-In-A Row Games from Ancient Egypt to the Modern Computer*
Zaslavsky	Claudia	1987	*Preparing Young Children For Math: A Book of Games*
Zaslavsky	Claudia	1993	*Multicultural Mathematics: Interdisciplinary Cooperative-Learning Activities*
Zaslavsky	Claudia	1994	*Fear of Math: How to Get over It and Get on With Your Life*
Zaslavsky	Claudia	1995	*The Multicultural Math Classroom: Bringing in the World*
Zaslavsky	Claudia	1996	*Multicultural Math: Hands-On Math Activities from Around the World*
Zaslavsky	Claudia	1998	*Math Games & Activities from Around the World*
Zaslavsky	Claudia	1999	*Africa Counts: Number and Pattern in African Cultures*
Zaslavsky	Claudia	2001	*Number Sense and Nonsense: Building Math Creativity and Confidence Through Number Play*
Zaslavsky	Claudia	2003	*More Math Games & Activities from Around the World*

APPENDIX 2
ETHICS OF SHARING

Appendix 2

Ethics of Sharing

Dr. Karenga has been instrumental in the development and adoption of a set of principles called The Ethics of Sharing, published by the African American Leadership Retreat Family, convened and nurtured by the Rev. Dr. Barbara Williams Skinner, in 2002. It states:

In the context of the best of African tradition, the African American Leadership Retreat Family proposes a national discourse and practice, which are self-consciously rooted in and reflective of a profound and ongoing commitment to:

1. the dignity and rights of the human person;
2. the well-being and flourishing of family and community:
3. the integrity and value of the environment; and
4. the reciprocal solidarity and cooperation for mutual benefit of humanity.

The central thrust of an ethical public philosophy and practice rooted in the Ethics of Sharing would include commitment to:

A. Shared Status – A mutual respect and recognition, rejecting all concepts and practices of superiority and inferiority of persons and peoples and upholding the principle of equal human and social worth for all.

B. Shared Knowledge – Access to the highest level and most current knowledge for the conception and achievement of maximum human flourishing.

C. Shared Space – Citizens and immigrants must share our country in an equitable and ethical way; the integrity of the environment must be respected; corporate private claims on public space and the environment must be restrained, and the isolation of the suburbs from the urban areas must be altered.

D. Shared Wealth (Economy) – Increasing beneficiaries of economic growth and expansion, promoting democratic decision-making in the economic process, and encouraging cooperative activities and shared interests. This is the principle of equitable distribution of wealth, based on the understanding that the right to a life in dignity includes the right to a decent life that provides basic necessities of food, clothing, shelter, health care, physical and economic security and education.

E. Shared Power – The ability to achieve social ends; meaningful and effective participation and decisions that determine our destiny and daily lives; and the ability to achieve substantial presence in critical political, economic and cultural arenas.

F. Shared Interests – This principle begins with a mutual commitment to the dignity and rights of the human person, the well-being and flourishing of family and community, the integrity and value of the environment, and the reciprocal solidarity and cooperation for mutual benefit of humanity.

G. Shared Responsibility – An active commitment to collective responsibility, including constant moral assessment, for building the good communities, society, and world in which we want and deserve to live.

The entire text of Ethics of Sharing can be found at www.ramonaedelin. com.

Notes

Introduction

1. Deaux, Kay & Gina Philogene. 2001. *Representations of the Social: Bridging Theoretical Traditions.* Oxford, UK: Blackwell Publishers.

Gourdine, A.K.M. 2002. *The Difference Place Makes: Gender, Sexuality, and Diaspora Identity.* Columbus: Ohio State University Press

Harper, Phillip Brian. 1998. *Are We Not Men?: Masculine Anxiety and the Problem of African-American Identity.* New York: Oxford University Press US.

Houk, James. 1993. "The Terminological Shift from 'Afro-American' to 'African-American:' Is the Field of Afro-American Anthropology Being Redefined?" *Human Organization,* 52(3):325-328

McClintock, Anne, Mufti, Aamir & Ella Shohat. 1997. "Dangerous Liaisons: Gender, Nation, and Postcolonial Perspectives." Cultural Politics Series, volume 11. Minneapolis, MN: University of Minnesota Press.

Philogene, Gina. 1999. *From Black to African American: A New Social Representation.* Westport, CT: Praeger.

Salikoko S. Mufwene, John R. Rickford, Guy Baile, & John Baugh. 1998. *African-American English: Structure, History, and* Use. New York: Routledge.

Smitherman, Geneva. 2000. *Talkin That Talk: Language, Culture, and Education in African America.* New York: Routledge.

Smitherman, Geneva. 1991. "What Is Africa to Me? Language, Ideology, and African Americans." American Speech, 66(2):115-32.

Zeigler, Mary B. & Viktor Osinubi. 2002. Theorizing the Postcoloniality of African American English. *Journal of Black Studies,* 32(5):588-609.

Newspapers (chronological order):

Specter, M. (1990, October 16). Shift to 'African American' May prove there is much in a name. *Washington Post*, p. A3

Lang, P. (1990, September 27). Name change links Blacks to homeland. *San Francisco Chronicle*, p. A1.

Smoothers, R. (1989, April 24). Blacks discussing routes to power. *New York Times*, p. A12.

Reynolds, B. (1989, April 20). New Black agenda: A whole generation is self-destructing. *USA Today*, p. 9A

Overbea, L. (1989, April 6). Blacks go for higher political office. *Christian Science Monitor*, p. 8.

Keene, L. (1989, March 22). Race debate: Will 'black' fade away? *San Diego Union-Tribune*, p. A-1.

Wilkerson, I. (1989, January 31). 'African American' favored by many of America's Blacks. *New York Times*, p. A1.

Myers, J. (1989, January 16). 'Black' may be replaced by 'African American.' *USA Today*, p. 9A.

Goodman, E. (1989, January 10). A change that makes emotional sense. *Boston Globe*, p. 15.

Ball, J. (1989, January 1). Rev. Jackson, others urge new name for blacks. *Boston Globe*, p. 1.

Associated Press. (1988, December 21). Jackson and others say 'Blacks' is passé. *New York Times*, p. A16.

ii. Visioning—Setting high level directions through visioning processes has emerged as a discipline in the last decade, fueled by increasing turbulence in the external environment. Industry shapers tend to do better than followers, especially when it's not clear what to follow. Being "visionary" is also a widely touted competency of leadership. Vision processes seek to create a compelling picture of desirable future states that often represent quantum changes from the past. They develop memorable imagery and stories about the nature and benefits of this future, and work backwards to understand the journey that could carry people to this vision. When visioning focuses on the generating short, exciting vision statements, it can result in banners and slogans so abstract they have little utility, especially if management doesn't truly "walk the talk". On the other hand, robust visioning processes that engage people in thorough exploration of possibilities, using different media to portray possible futures, and engaging leadership directly in the process can be extraordinarily energizing for an organization. It can help an organization break out of overly constrained view of the future and is a powerful way of tying values to action.

http:www.nea.gov/resources/lessons/grove.html

Chapter 2: Defining and Establishing the Cultural Context

1. Maulana Karenga's definition in the second edition of *Introduction to Black Studies* is very helpful. His kawaida theory "defines culture in the broadest sense to equate it with all the thought and activity of a given people or society" and focuses on seven areas of analysis and problem solving: religion, history, social organization, economic organization, political organization, creative production and ethos. (p.26)

2. The NAACP Board of Directors codified this consensus in a formal statement upon acceptance of his resignation in 1934. *(Autobiography,* p. 299)

3. (W.E.B. Du Bois From "The Conservation of Races" provided by Julius Lester in *The Seventh Son,* Vol. 1., pp 176-188.)

4. Harold Cruse maintained that "as long as [African American] cultural identity is in question or open to self-doubt, then there can be no positive identification with the real demands of his political and economic existence." Maulana Karenga, p. 277, *Introduction to Black Studies.*

5. John U. Ogbu, Minority Education and Caste (New York, San Francisco, London: Academic Press, Subsidiary of Harcourt Brace Jovanovich, Publishers: 1978. A Carnegie Council on Children Monograph).

Chapter 3: That Was Then, This Is Now

1. Basil Davidson, in "The Ancient World and Africa: Whose Roots?" states, The racism that we know was born [in about 1830] in Europe and America from the cultural need to justify doing to black people, doing to Africans, what could not morally or legally be done to white people.... To justify the enslavement of Africans, in short, it was culturally necessary to believe, or be able to believe, that Africans were inherently and naturally less than human but were beings of a somehow sub-human, non-human, nature. That was the cultural basis, in this context, of the slave trade and of the modern imperialism in Africa, which followed the slave trade. The racism that we know, accordingly, was altogether different from ancient xenophobia...: its core and motivation were to act as a weapon of dispossession and exploitation. (Ivan Van Sertima, editor, *Egypt Revisited* (New Brunswick and London: Transaction Publishers, 1989, p.40)9

2. "Social organization occurs among men, animals and insects. It occurs at the smallest levels of society, the three-person unit, and at the largest level, that of the mass society. It is carried in the head, and it is exhibited in the behavior of the individuals comprising the society, groups, and subgroups. It occurs spontaneously, and it may be enforced by various instruments of coercion—law, threat, weapons, punishment. It is the first, and the foremost, construct involved in the understanding of what transforms a collectivity of individuals into an operating group. For social organization is more than an aggregate of individuals: it is an ongoing social system governed by rules of dominance and subordination, rules of the appropriate and the inappropriate, rules of right and wrong. These rules emerge from and control the interactive patterns." *Mirror of Man*, edited by Jane Dabaghian (Boston: Little, Brown & Company, 1970) p. 24.10.

3. See Du Bois, *Dusk of Dawn,* p.150, for elucidation of the affirmation that, "Great as has been the human advance in the last thousand years, it is, so far as native human ability, so far as intellectual gift and moral courage are concerned, nothing as compared with any one of ten and more millenniums before, far back in the forests of tropical Africa and in hot India, where brown and black humanity first fought climate and disease and bugs, and beasts; where man dared simply to live and propagate himself. There was the hardest and greatest

struggle in all the human world." See also *Darkwater*, p.166, '...as if the great black race in passing up the steps of human culture gave the world, not only the Iron Age, the cultivation of the soil, and the domestication of animals, but also in peculiar emphasis, the mother-idea."

4. Du Bois found in Karenga, op. cit., p. 89, "The history of civilization which began in Egypt was not so much a matter of dynasties and dates. It was an attempt to settle the problems of living together, of government, defense, religion, family, property, science and art."

5. See, among other good sources, Lerone Bennett, Jr., *Before the Mayflower* (Baltimore: Penguin Books, Inc., 1966, pp. 13 -28.)

6. (New York: Vintage Books, a Division of Random House, 1969, copyright 1947, Alfred A. Knopf)

7. Sterling Stuckey, *The Ideological Origins of Black Nationalism*, (Boston: Beacon Press, 1972). p.36

8 Ibid. p. 46

9. Ibid. p. 178

10. W.E.B. Du Bois, *Souls of Black Folk*, (New, (New York: Dover Publications, Inc., 1994, originally published: Chicago: A.C. McClurg, 1903) p. 9

Chapter 4: Vision and Purpose
1. Well-ordered definitions of the good, both profoundly spiritual and practical, governed the lives of ancient Nubians and Demeans and the workings of their state. Written treatises and enduring evidence of this body of knowledge reveal some of its dimensions as an active social ethic. Maat was the Egyptian moral and spiritual way. (Runoko Rashidi, in Van Sertima, *Egypt Revisited*, pp.105-117) Its system of teachings addressed questions of relationships of humanity to individuals, to family and community, to the state (Van Sertima, op. cit., citing Karenna, pp.352-399) and to the Higher Power. Righteousness, respect for each person, generosity, care for those who need it, truth and honesty are among its tenets. Karenna

maintains that the requirements of Maat informed and helped to shape the just society that was achieved. Moreover, Maat has informed and helped to shape the Judea-Christian principles to which many claim allegiance today.

2. Du Bois, *The Gift of Black Folk: Negroes in the Making of America* (Boston: Stratford Company, 1924, pp. 66-7)

Chapter 5: Connect The Dots
1. The *Sebait of Ptah-Hotep* (5:1-4) as referenced in Karenga, *op. cit.*, p. 358.

Chapter 6: Self-Knowledge, Self-Love
1. Please see the elegant accounts of Professor Sterling Stuckey in his The Ideological Origins of Black Nationalism (Boston: Beacon Press, 1972). There, he posits that "...the desire for autonomy among a significant number of blacks, surely as old as the 1600's, may well have crystallized into ideology some years before the crucial decade of the 1850's." (p. 2)

2. "... the African village, because of geography and climate, because perhaps of some curious inner tenacity and strength of tradition, persisted and did on a small scale what the world has continually attempted on a wider scale and never satisfactorily accomplished. The African village socialized the individual completely, and yet because the village was small this socialization did not submerge and kill individuality". (Du Bois, "What is Civilization: Africa's Answer" in Meyer Weinberg, *W.E.B. Du Bois A Reader* (NY, Evanston, London: Harper and Row, 1970, p. 125)

3. "Culture has proven to be an adaptive mechanism in the evolution of man as a species. Where other animals adapt genetically to their environments, man, through culture, adapts his environment to his needs. Since culture is learned behavior, the evolution of man's culture has been bought at the expense of instinctive behavior. All societies...control the major part of instinctive behavior: each culture determines how, when, why, where, with whom and under what conditions the instincts - such as sexual and/or procreative instincts -may be gratified." Dabaghian, *op. cit.*, pp. 25-26.

4. Please see Edwin J. Nichols, Ph.D., Cultural Foundations for Teaching Black Children, and The Philosophical Aspects of Cultural Difference.

Chapter 7: What Can We Do?
1. Follow these links for information about national organizations that define and pursue policy agendas on behalf of African-descended people: http://www.ncnw.org/centers/research.htm
        http://www.thecongressionalblackcaucus.com/
        http://www.transafricaforum.org/policy-overview
        http://www.naacp.org/legal/index.htm
        http://www.blackleadershipforum.org/reports.html
        http://www.nlc.org/insidenlc/constituencygroups/nbc
          leo/822.aspx
        http://www.nul.org/.

2. Stuckey, op. cit., p. 118, "10 Letters by Augustine" from the "Colored American," December 2, 1837.

Chapter 8: Achieving Our Collective Greatness Now
1. Please see the following:
        The Covenant, Introduction by Tavis Smiley, Third World Press© 2006 The Smiley Group.

        The Covenant in Action, Compiled by Tavis Smiley, Smiley Books an imprint of Hay House, Inc. Carlsbad, California Sydney, London, Johannesburg, Vancouver, Hong Kong, New Delhi, 2006.

        The Hidden Cost of Being African American How Wealth Perpetuates Inequality, Thomas M. Shapiro, © 2004 by Thomas M. Shapiro, published by Oxford University Press, Inc. New York.

        Black Wealth/White Wealth A New Perspective on Racial Inequality, Melvin L. Oliver and Thomas M. Shapiro, © 1995 by Routledge, NY.

        The Color of Wealth The Story Behind the U.S. Racial Wealth Divide by United for a Fair Economy, Published in the United States by The New Press, NY 2006, Distributed by W.W. Norton & Company, Inc., NY.

2. Please follow this link for studies on structural racism: http://www. aspeninstitute.org/policywork/community-change/structural-racism-resources.

3. [Abraham] Maslow has set up a hierarchy of five levels of basic needs. Beyond these needs, higher levels of needs exist. These include needs for understanding, esthetic appreciation and purely spiritual needs. In the levels of the five basic needs, the person does not feel the second need until the demands of the first have been satisfied, nor the third until the second has been satisfied, and so on. Maslow's basic needs are as follows:

Physiological Needs
These are biological needs. They consist of needs for oxygen, food, water, and a relatively constant body temperature. They are the strongest needs because if a person were deprived of all needs, the physiological ones would come first in the person's search for satisfaction.

Safety Needs
When all physiological needs are satisfied and are no longer controlling thoughts and behaviors, the needs for security can become active. Adults have little awareness of their security needs except in times of emergency or periods of disorganization in the social structure (such as widespread rioting). Children often display the signs of insecurity and the need to be safe.

Needs of Love, Affection and Belongingness
When the needs for safety and for physiological well-being are satisfied, the next class of needs for love, affection and belongingness can emerge. Maslow states that people seek to overcome feelings of loneliness and alienation. This involves both giving and receiving love, affection and the sense of belonging.

Needs for Esteem
When the first three classes of needs are satisfied, the needs for esteem can become dominant. These involve needs for both self-esteem and for the esteem a person gets from others. Humans have a need for a stable, firmly based, high level of self-respect, and respect from others. When these needs are satisfied, the person feels self-confident and valuable as

a person in the world. When these needs are frustrated, the person feels inferior, weak, helpless and worthless.

Needs for Self-Actualization
When all of the foregoing needs are satisfied, then and only then are the needs for self-actualization activated. Maslow describes self-actualization as a person's need to be and do that which the person was "born to do." "A musician must make music, an artist must paint, and a poet must write." These needs make themselves felt in signs of restlessness. The person feels on edge, tense, lacking something, in short, restless. If a person is hungry, unsafe, not loved or accepted, or lacking self-esteem, it is very easy to know what the person is restless about. It is not always clear what a person wants when there is a need for self-actualization. from *Psychology: The Search for Understanding* by Janet A. Simons, Donald B. Irwin and Beverly A. Drinnien. West Publishing Company, New York, 1987.

4. An excellent reference is Niara Sudarkasa: http:Uwww.jendajournal. com/issue5/sudarkasa.htm

JENdA: A Journal of Culture and African Women Studies ISSN: 1530-5686 Conceptions of Motherhood in Nuclear and Extended Families, with Special Reference to Comparative Studies Involving African Societies.

5. For resources on the vitally important topic of Parenting: http://www.google.com/search?q=parenting+african+american+chil dren&rls=com.microsoft:enus:IE-Address&ie=UTF-8&oe=UTF-8&sourceid=ie7&rlz=117DMUS.

6. Charter schools are public schools that are open to all students, regardless of income, race, or religion. They are independently designed and operated and committed to improving the academic achievement of all children. As schools of choice, charter schools are highly responsive to the needs of students and communities, charter schools are extremely appealing to families from all backgrounds, particularly those dissatisfied with their neighborhood traditional public school. (http://www. publiccharters.org/aboutschools/benefits).

    http://www.publiccharters.org/aboutschools /factsheet
    http://www.publiccharters.org/aboutschools

7. Assess the law in your state against this model legislation: ModelLaw P7-wCVR.pdf (2.67 MB).

8. senate.gov!reference/...lkids!HowGovtWorksBooks.htm.

9. Please see Appendix for the text of the Ethics of Sharing

10. Job 22:28 "Thou shalt also decree a thing, and it shall be established unto thee; and the light shall shine upon thy ways." American King James Version.

11. See the New Jim Crow by Michelle Alexander:
        http://www.newjimcrow.com/

12. See this report from The Sentencing Project:
http://sentencing.typepad.com/sentencing law and policy/2009/04/new-report-from-thesentencing-project-on-the-drug-wars-racial-dynamics.html

13. First Lady Michelle Obama has defined and is promoting a health initiative that includes reducing national levels of childhood obesity: http://www.mediabistro.com/fishbowlny!first-ladymichelle-obama-takes-her-health-initiative-to-five-meredith-magazinesb158871\

14. http://www.connectccp.org/resources/27community.pdf
        http:Uwww.fieldmuseum.org/calumet/assetmap.html
        http://www.urban-advantage.com/SoulsvilleUSA

Ramona Hoage Edelin is a scholar, activist and executive consultant with forty years of experience in leadership to uplift and advance African Americans and the economically disadvantaged. A Phi Beta Kappa graduate of Fisk University, she earned masters and doctorate degrees in philosophy from the University of East Anglia in Norwich, England and Boston University, respectively. After founding the Department of African American Studies at Northeastern University in 1973, she served the National Urban Coalition for 21 years, the last 10 as President and CEO; and she directed the Congressional Black Caucus Foundation from 1998-2003. She has served as Executive Director of the District of Columbia Association of Chartered Public Schools since 2006. A nationally respected lecturer, her media presentations include network, public and cable television, radio, print and other published venues.